1

If you have no confidence in self, you are twice defeated in the race of life. With confidence you've won even before you've started.

---- **Marcus Garvey**

First Thing First: Why own a Non-medical Home Care Business?

You probably already have some idea of the rewards available in starting a Non-Medical Home Care business if you are reading this guide. You may be sharing in these rewards already. Just in case you are not familiar with the scope of the Non-Medical Home Care business, let's take a minute to expand your view of this incredible business.

Non-medical home care: What is it?

Home care in the United States is a diverse and dynamic service industry. Approximately 20,000 providers deliver home care services to 7.6 million individuals who require services because of acute illness, long-term health conditions, permanent disability, or terminal illness. Annual expenditures for home health care are projected to be $58.3 billion in 2024. Home care is a broad term that describes a wide variety of health and health related services provided in the home setting. Home care is health care brought to your home to maintain or restore your health and well-being.

Non-Medical Home Care providers represent a rapidly growing trend to allow people needing help to remain in their home or in the community. The services offered may include:

- Meal preparation
- Administration of medication
- Surveillance
- Secure environment
- Assistance with activities of daily living (ambulatory care, bathing, grooming, feeding)
- Laundry, changing linens, ironing
- Entertainment, recreational activities
- Companionship
- Incontinent care
- Handyman services
- Light housekeeping
- Respite for family caregivers
- Errands and shopping
- Reading email or letters
- Overseeing home deliveries
- Dealing with vendors
- Transportation services
- Care of house plants

- 24-hour emergency response

These providers receive reimbursement directly from families; from other care providers whom they subcontract for or from long term care insurance.

Growth Trends in the industry

Seniors are one of the fastest growing population groups in the United States. The senior population has grown about twice as fast as the overall population since the early 1980s. The growth is also expected to continue early in the second decade of the new century when baby boomers turn 65. Seniors aged 85 and over are the fastest growing segment of the overall senior population. Consequently, the demand for Non-Medical Home Care services is also growing.

With regards to housing, seniors have to face numerous challenges. More and more seniors share a vast range of interests and needs. They also have variable physical limitations and health conditions. Partnerships between the public, non-profit and private sectors are being organized to offer housing services adapted to seniors' specific needs. Some concerned citizens are looking for means to offer a service in their own community that would allow long-time residents to continue living in their community.

The senior population of the United States is expected to grow rapidly. By the year 2035, those over 65 years old will make up nearly 30 percent of the total population, which reflects growth of 37 percent from 2010 to 2035.

While Non-Medical Home Care businesses serve the senior population, they are simultaneously serving informal caregivers. The 9 million adult children who are raising children while caring for aged parents are called the "Sandwich Generation," 40 percent of which are between the ages of 35 and 49, according to the American Association of Retired Persons (AARP) and the National Alliance for Caregiving (NAC). Almost 40 percent of the senior population currently relies on a working son or daughter, according to a survey by SCAN, a social health maintenance organization in Long Beach, Calif.

In 2019 approximately 25 percent of all workers in the United States cared for an ailing parent or relative, and by 2025 the portion of workers who are caregivers is expected to rise to 45 percent, according to the Families and Work Institute in New York.

The careers and health of caregivers are often harmed by their efforts to provide Home Care, as reported by Industry Week Daily News. Five out of six American workers who work outside the home are forced to quit, retire early, cut back work hours, take a leave of absence, take sick leave, or use up their vacation time in order to care for elderly family members. An estimated 22.4 million families (almost one-fourth of all households) provides 80 percent of the long-term care for the elderly. Twenty-nine percent of caregivers passed up promotions, training, and new jobs. About one-quarter reported that care giving prevented them from gaining new skills. Nearly 75 percent said that caring for their elders had harmed their own health.

- *The average senior is spending approximately $5,600 per month for care in a private room in a nursing home.* MetLife Mature Market Institute

- *There are currently 36 Million Seniors in the U.S. Over the next few decades that number is projected to exceed 70 Million.* **U.S. Census Bureau**

- *It is estimated that annual expenditures on home care exceeded $50 billion in 2025.* **National Association of Home Care**

- *In 2020, 37% of all U.S. Workers faced more concern in caring for a parent than caring for a child.* **Aragon Consulting**

- *More than 12 million Americans require some long-term care. As many as 6 out of every 10 Americans have family members or friends requiring long-term care services. 8 out of every 10 would prefer to have care provided at their family member's home.* **U.S. General Accounting Office**

- *The fastest-growing occupation through 2030 will be Personal/Home Care Aides. Faster than Systems Analyst, Computer Engineers, Medical Assistants, Paralegals, Occupational Therapy Aides or any other occupation.* **Bureau of Labor Statistics**

- *Seniors prefer to remain in the privacy and comfort of their own home versus moving to a nursing home or assisted living center.* **Ask Any Senior**

Over the past 15 years, home care has evolved and grown by responding to changes that have occurred in the acute care sector (bed closures, increase in ambulatory care clinics, and day surgery) or limitations in the long term care sector (waiting lists for beds, limited availability). Home care is one of the fastest growing sectors of health spending. Public expenditures for home care have increased from just over $205 million in 2010-2015 (.6 % of the total public health care expenditures) to $2.5 billion in 2022-2023 (3.5 % of the total public health care expenditures).

Why clients hire non-medical Home Care providers?

The non-medical home care business has taken off due to two factors: lower costs than nursing home care and the preference of seniors to remain independent. According to the National Council on Independent Living, 18.9 percent of the current residents of Medicaid or Medicare-certified nursing homes would prefer to return to the community. The same report cites $102,200 as the average cost of nursing home services per person each year. The average cost of in-home, non-medical caretaking is $19,500.

According to AARP, as Americans age, most will remain in their own homes. Nearly 7 out of 10 older Americans own their own residence and most have no plans to move.

As a result, fewer seniors are getting the help they need with simple daily functioning. For example, in 2015, 80 percent of seniors needing help to prepare their meals reported that someone was available to help them; by 2019, that had dropped to just 60 percent, according to the National Council on Aging. Overall, from 2010 to

2019 there was a significant decrease in the number of seniors who reported that they had spouses, relatives, friends or neighbors to provide personal care or assistance.

Today, an ever-increasing senior population has fewer resources available to help them with the daily tasks of living. At the same time, older adults have longer life expectancies than ever before.

By remaining in their own homes, seniors can retain an important sense of independence. It is also psychologically beneficial for older adults to remain in familiar surroundings. While their well-meaning children may wish to put them in a retirement home, the fact is that forced relocation can cause some seniors to feel disoriented, depressed and confused.

In addition, there is a significant difference between a senior who simply needs help with personal care and one who requires medical assistance. A relatively healthy older adult who is placed in a facility with those who are far more infirm will feel out of place in such surroundings.

Remaining as independent as possible can boost a senior's overall sense of well-being. Staying in their own home is, in most cases, far more preferable (as well as less costly) than relocating to an assisted living facility. It gives them a sense of empowerment, and allows them to retain close friendships with neighbors.

Until recently, however, few choices were available to seniors who wished to remain at home but did not require medical assistance. Medical Home Care can be costly, since most professionals must be registered nurses or nurses' assistants. In addition, they may balk at performing light housekeeping tasks. Finally, they rarely have the opportunity to build long relationships with their clients. Often a different professional appears every week, which is disorienting to seniors and prevents establishing a bond with their caregiver.

Your business, Non-medical Home Care, in contrast, is designed to help the older adult with the tasks of everyday living. Non-medical caregivers do not assist with medical procedures, and since they are not registered nurses or medical personnel, their hourly rate is not as high. They also offer the opportunity for steady companionship, as they are generally assigned to specific clients on a long-term basis, enabling a friendship to grow.

Non-medical caregivers can also form strong bonds with the senior's family. Indeed, in order to ensure a good match, it is key that the caregiver interviews with the family as well as the client.

These caregivers can help seniors maintain their independence by taking over the daily tasks that become increasingly difficult with age. They can take the client grocery shopping or to the bank, prepare meals, do light housekeeping and provide daily conversation and companionship.

It is important to note that some Non-Medical Home Care agencies offer companion care only, while others offer both companion and personal care. It is important to check with your state-licensing agency to obtain the appropriate license for the services you will offer. Not all Non-Medical Home Care agencies can perform personal care services without a licensed.

In the end, Non-Medical Home Care is an option that allows the senior to remain in the home without feeling overwhelmed. The senior receives the assistance and companionship required, and the family enjoys peace of mind that a beloved parent, aunt or uncle is not struggling with the simple tasks of everyday living. It is a "win-win" situation for all.

What Types of services you can provide.

Each Non-Medical Home Care company will offer minimum services, which can vary from one to four hours per day. Some companies will offer up to twenty-four hour care and even live-ins. All of the services listed below are non-medical in nature. The following is a partial list of services you can provide:

- Respite care – relief for the primary caregiver

- Assist with bathing…in and out of tub or shower

- Prepare meals

- Medication reminders

- Answer the phone, read mail

- Daily "Care Call" – daily phone call to check on client.

- Supervise home maintenance such as gardeners, repairmen, plumbers

- Provide companionship and conversation

- Read aloud, play cards or board games

- Lawn mowing

- Snow removal from sidewalks and drives

- Light Housekeeping

- Organize closets

- Change linens

- Light laundry

- Errands and Transportation

- Grocery and other shopping trips

- Pick up prescriptions or transport to the pharmacy

- Take to doctor appointments and take notes during visit if needed

- Theater and movie events

- Drive to family or other gatherings

- Buy stamps or mail packages

- Accompany to church

Do you have what it takes to run a Non-Medical Home Care business?

Starting a Non-Medical Home Care business can be a rewarding undertaking, but it comes with its challenges. Before starting a business it is wise to do your research. Ask yourself if you are truly suited for entrepreneurship and understand that significant effort may be required. You should thoroughly enjoy the business of helping other people and you must believe in your service; it may consume much of your time, especially in the start-up phase. Starting a business is risky at best, but your chances of making it succeed will be better if you understand the problems you'll meet and work out as many of them as you can before you start.

Non-Medical Home Care services are:

- Demanding physically - expect long working days, including some part of the nights

- Demanding emotionally - you have to deal with often lonely and frequently ill people much of the time

- Challenging - you must excel in many areas such as food preparation, services, management, marketing, meeting people, purchasing, inventory control and personnel administration

- Often involving numerous disciplines, such as finance, accounting, social work, medicine, psychology, law, fitness, nutrition, recreational, restoration and nursing

Rewarding, but it can be a negative experience if you are not comfortable working with the elderly - especially as their mental and physical health deteriorate

Since Non-Medical Home Care is a very demanding multi-disciplinary activity, there are many questions you should ask yourself and others before making a decision to enter this industry. Such questions might include:

What needs to happen in order to prompt you to take action? Is self-employment something that has recently occurred to you or has it been building up for some time? Who could influence your decision? Who would you need to consult with? Whose support do you need? Is it just some encouragement or advice you're after before you can believe it's possible?

The answers start with you. In the early days, your Non-Medical Home Care business will be very much a reflection of your personality and just getting through the start-up process will depend on your ability to handle all the issues that arise. Think about the skills you have to help you and to give your business an advantage. Make a thorough assessment of your weaknesses as well, but don't be discouraged, nobody's perfect! If you can think of areas to improve, gaining some new skills could turn out to be the trigger you need to get started on developing your Non-Medical Home Care business. And if your weaknesses can't be improved there are always ways of working round them.

Better Business Tip

Do something you love. If you're in a business you hate, then it's a good bet you won't be successful. Identify your true talents and skills, and get into a business that makes the most of them.

The saying, "If you do what you love, the money will follow," is true.

The following simple exercise is designed to help you draw up a list of your key strengths and weaknesses.

This is a classic technique used by management consultants. Simply take a blank piece of paper, draw a line down the center, and head the two columns 'strengths' and 'weaknesses'.

List your key strengths and weaknesses as honestly as you can. It might help to split them into three key categories: business skills, people skills and problem-solving skills.

Richard Greenstead, author of <u>Go It Alone</u>, says: This process - of determining your own values and virtues - is fundamental to your own business success. Before you can become successful in the Non-Medical Home Care industry, you must have a very clear idea of the type of person you are, and what attributes you can most effectively use to be successful.

2

Do the things you know, and you shall learn
the truth you need to know.
--- **George Macdonald**

Researching Your Target Market

Define Your Target Market

Successful businesses have extensive knowledge about
their clients and their competitors. Acquiring accurate
and specific information about your potential clients
and competitors is a critical first step in market
investigation and development of a marketing plan.

In developing a marketing plan, your primary functions are to understand the needs and desires of your clients, select the Non-Medical Home Care services that will meet their needs, develop promotional material that will make them aware and ensure service delivery.

It is important to clearly define your target market. If a banker or potential investor asks you "Who is your target Market?" and you reply with "Everyone and Anyone" they immediately know you didn't do your homework, causing many to question the validity of your business plan in its entirety. General questions to ask about your Non-Medical Home Care business can include:

- What type of services do I want to provide?

- Are there any competitors in my area and, if so, can my services be distinct?

- How many older people live in my area? How many live alone?

- Do I understand the needs of elderly people?

- Do I know the related services offered in my region?

- How many clients do I want at one time?

- Do I have the time, money and abilities for such a business?

- Is the location appropriate for such a business?

- Should I consult with professionals? Which ones?

- What type of professional help will I need?

- Is there a need to have a market study done?

- What regulations are involved?

- What happens when a person living under my care dies?

- Is there a public transportation system in my area? Do I want to provide transportation services?

 Non-Medical Home Care business owners know how important it is to be familiar with client needs and preferences. But having a general idea of what clients want from your business is not enough to create truly effective advertising and marketing campaigns. Entrepreneurs must take that knowledge to the next level and define target audiences to connect with the clients they want to reach.

Target audiences are distinct groups or segments of clients. And clearly defining your business' target audiences will help you promote the aspects of your business that are most relevant to each group.

Most businesses cater to a variety of clients. Some marketing strategies will be relevant to all those segments, but knowing each target audience well will help you deliver your marketing messages in a way clients will respond to best.

On a wider scale, you can segment your clients using demographics. Demographic information categorizes people in categories like age, location, occupation, sex and income.

Questions to ask yourself about your clients can include:

- What is the age range and median age?

- Is the group primarily male or female?

- Are they urban dwellers or suburbanites?

- Are they highly educated?

- What are their special interests or hobbies?

- What is their income range?

As a Non-Medical Home Care business owner, it is up to you to understand what the motivations are that drive your clients. This isn't always as easy as it sounds, and most people don't take this past the first level. In the case of Non-Medical Home Care, the obvious answer is that they are looking for someone to take care of their family members. But this is only the service that they want; it is not what motivates them. Ask yourself why they want this, and you will find that these motivations are more personal than shopping for an available service.

Identifying Your Potential Clients

One of the most important factors for determining market feasibility is the customer base for your Non-Medical Home Care service. Understanding your clients means understanding their reasons for buying your services. It is critical to identify the group of people with:

1. The greatest need for the Non-Medical Home Care services.
2. The willingness to purchase your services.

Identifying potential clients and their locations helps businesses determine if these clients can be reached. If they can be reached, we can continue to determine the market feasibility of the project. If not, then not much time, effort or money was used. Starting your feasibility assessments with client identification will saves you money in the long run.

Identifying clients requires answering three basic questions.
    1. Who are your clients?
    2. Where are your clients?
    3. Can you access your clients?

There are two steps to identify your clients: qualitative assessment and quantitative assessment. To identify a base of clients qualitatively, you must consider the previous mentioned characteristics that your potential clients will have in common.

- Demographic variables such as age, income, education, gender, occupation and family size.

- Geographic variables such as urban, suburban, rural, regional population distribution and city size.

- Personality variables such as social class, values and life-styles.

- Behavior variables such as benefits desired from the service, usage rate and the level of brand loyalty expressed toward similar services.

Once you know what attributes your typical client will possess, you can determine the number of people who fit the description. The number of potential clients must be large enough to generate a satisfactory volume of sales. If not, the business will not succeed and nothing else in the market feasibility study, business plan, or marketing plan matters.

There likely will be a large number of potential clients in your marketplace. However, no one business can be all things to all people. In order to reach potential clients effectively and efficiently, you must select a specific market that you believe has the potential to be the most profitable for you. For start-up businesses, this often involves limiting market potential geographically due to capital constraints and familiarity with customer base. Although there may be markets with greater profit-potential that are not located within your business' region, it will be extremely expensive to offer your services to these markets. When all costs are considered, markets within a smaller distance of your business may be the most profitable for you.

Now that you know what your typical client profile is and how many people fit the description, you must identify where these clients are located. Part of the answer may come from the geographic variables determined in the first step of the process. However, now you must also determine the most concentrated geographic areas of individuals who fit your typical client profile. You can find this information by using the Internet or your local library. Sources such as the U.S. Census Bureau and the Office of Social and Economic Data Analysis (OSEDA) publish population breakdowns and other demographic information by regions. Once you have determined areas with the highest concentration of your potential clients, you must consider where your business is located and decide where you want to market your Non-Medical Home Care service based on your ability to reach these consumers.

The final question you must answer is whether or not you can access your clients. There are a variety of factors that may interfere with your ability to reach potential buyers: establishing brand recognition and market saturation levels, just to name a few.

Even if your potential market is huge, it won't matter if you can't access it. For example, suppose you decide to open your Non-Medical Home Care business in a large metropolitan area with a high market saturation level. While this is a large market, there may be a lot of "players" dominating it. This may cause difficulty with gaining brand recognition with so many competitors. However, if you come in with unique services or better pricing, you will be much more likely to gain brand recognition because your services will stand out. Knowing who your clients are, where they are located and if you can access them is key to determining the potential success of your business.

Identify & Analyze Your Competition

Before you launch your Non-Medical Home Care business, you better know what you're up against. If you don't size up the competition, you're likely to be sideswiped.

This market research effort doesn't have to be scientific or involve expensive studies (although you can go that route). Often you can get results that will point your start-up efforts in the right direction by simply identifying the competition and talking to your potential clients.

Even though Non-Medical Home Care is a growing
industry, opening up a new business will not be unique.
It's more than likely that you'll be setting up in
competition with other Non-Medical Home Care
businesses, some of which will be established and doing
well. Winning business from them won't be easy, so to
make a success of your new venture you'll need to think
about what makes you and your company special. What
will persuade clients to come to you? What will make
them use your services and what will make them
continue to use your services for years to come?

Every business has competition. Companies stating
they have no competition lose credibility in the eyes of a
lender. It is important to identify the strengths and
weaknesses of your main competitions. You may want
to provide a detailed assessment of your top 3-5
competitors, more if necessary.

Provide a detailed assessment including:

- A summary of their services. Provide strengths
  and weaknesses. How do their Non-Medical
  Home Care services compare to yours?

- What is the Strength of the competition? Provide
  sales estimates. Do they have the same target
  market or operate in your niche? What are the
  company strengths and weaknesses including
  their Non-Medical Home Care services?

- What is the impact on your company? Why will
  people buy your Non-Medical Home Care services
  over the competition? What makes your Non-
  Medical Home Care services different?

- Determine your competitors' size, including how
  many employees they have. Survey their pricing,
  hours of operation and find out where they
  advertise.

The next step is to identify and provide a detailed assessment (similar to that completed for your primary competitor) for all other competitors. Ensure you identify all major competitors and alternative services that clients may use instead of utilizing your business.

Here are five easy tools that will help you pin down your competitors and refine your business:

- If you're searching based on geography, start with the phone book, newspaper or online. One of the best online sources is Switchboard. Search simultaneously by category and by distance or Zip code.

- You can do a thorough online search using any of the major search engines.

- Examine the competition by North American Industry Classification System (NAICS) code. The Census Bureau uses these codes to report on businesses, including such information as payroll size. You can access the census data yourself at the U.S. Census Bureau Web site.

- Visit your city or county planning office. Virtually every county has one, which, among other things, compiles information about local business. As a taxpayer, the information there is yours to use free of charge.

- Check out one of the various business lists produced by InfoUSA, with details on millions of companies in the United States and Canada, including addresses, telephone numbers, employment data, key contact and title, primary Standard Industrial Classification (SIC) code, actual and estimated financial data on companies. Data is compiled through a continuous updating cycle of compilation from print sources (including more than 5,000 yellow-page books) and telephone interviews capturing additional data. This information is pricey but useful. Try your public library before you buy.

After you've got the cold, hard statistics, go to the people you expect to buy your Non-Medical Home Care services. And don't just ask your friends or your mother-in-law or anyone else who has a vested interested in your success.
If you already have clients, talk to them. If you're starting a new business, you can conduct a market survey. Below are some questions you can ask.

- Do you have a need for Non-Medical Home Care services?

- What need do you have that would prompted you to seek out Non-Medical Home Care services?

- When and how often do you use Non-Medical Home Care services?

- How many people did you talk to or visit before you bought the service?

- What motivated you to choose the company you did?

Getting answers to questions like these may require a bribe. One good approach is to offer a gift certificate in return for cooperation. It doesn't have to be much. A $5 McDonald's coupon, for instance, can buy you a little time and lots of goodwill and information.

You might consider holding a focus group and feeding people lunch in return for answering your questions.

This also will help them remember you once you launch your service.

In any case, don't forget to follow-up and send the person you talked to a thank you. That will give them one more reason to remember you.

Once you identify the market and survey the competition, look for ways to differentiate yourself. Ask yourself what your company can provide that will make it essential to key clients. It is important to do a few things well and don't try to take on the world. Above all else, be ethical and professional. Often it comes down to the intangibles, "Do they like you? Do they trust you? Do they think you know what you're doing"?

Your Pricing Strategy

Your pricing strategy involves determining how you will price your Non-Medical Home Care services; the price you charge has to be competitive but still allow you to make a reasonable profit.

The keyword here is "reasonable", you can charge any price you want to, but for every service there's a limit to how much the consumer is willing to pay. Your pricing strategy needs to take this consumer threshold into account.

The most common question about the pricing strategy is, "How do you know what price to charge?"

Basically you set your pricing through a process of calculating your costs, estimating the benefits to clients, and comparing your services, and prices to others that are similar.

Set your pricing by examining how much it cost you to provide your services and adding a fair price for the benefits that the clients will enjoy. Examining what others are charging for similar services will guide you when you're figuring out what a "fair" price for such benefits would be. You may find it useful to conduct a Breakeven Analysis.

The pricing strategy you outline will answer the following questions:
What is the cost of your services? Make sure you include all your fixed and variable costs when you're calculating this; the cost of labor and materials are obvious, but you may also need to include administrative costs, for example.

How does the pricing of your Non-Medical Home Care services compare to the market price of similar services?

Explain how the pricing of your services is competitive. For instance, if the price you plan to charge is lower, why are you able to do this? If it were higher, why would your clients be willing to pay more? This is where the "strategy" part of the pricing strategy comes into play; will your business be more competitive if you charge more, less, or the same as your competitors and why? What kind of ROI (Return On Investment) are you expecting with this pricing strategy, and within what time frame?

Determining your Pricing

Consumers are willing to pay for exceptional service. Your Non-Medical Home Care clients are no different. Let's say you can offer high quality Non-Medical Home Care services. At what price are your services correctly positioned? At a price that emphasizes the value of your services over cost. First try to determine what a client would be willing to pay for your services before you figure your actual cost. Think of the benefits your services will deliver and the quality of your expertise. Of course expenses must be met and a reasonable mark-up should be included, but why have a give-away-the-store mentality by setting the price of your services so low because overhead costs seem relatively negligible?

Yet what if you continually find yourself having to defend the price of your services? The client may be telling you there isn't enough value for what you're charging. You may need to rethink the services you are providing at that price point, your reputation, or other factors that could be affecting the client's perception of your services.

Now here's an interesting scenario: There's this new guy down the street. He's just set up shop and he's advertising the same services you provide at price points that cut your prices to pieces. Since you don't live in a vacuum, what are you going to do?

First, don't overreact. Don't worry about losing the consumers that are so price sensitive. After all, if you price your services too low you may get more business but you'll lose the profit from the less sensitive ones -- and they're out there by the droves! And if you do react to the challenge to compete on price alone, you as well as your competitor will both lose.

Secondly, don't forget to address your client's perception of your business while making an honest evaluation of your services. And when setting a fair price, emphasize value over cost. Just remember: A client will usually pay for the Non-Medical Home Care services they need and want whatever the selling price.

3

Man cannot discover new oceans unless he has the courage to lose sight of the shore.

--- **Andre Gide**

Create Your Company Identity

Planning your Non-Medical Home Care Business

What is a Business Plan? A business plan is a recognized management tool used by successful and/or prospective businesses of all sizes to document business objectives and to propose how these objectives will be attained within a specific period of time. It is a written document, which describes who you are, what you plan to achieve, where your business will be located, when you expect to get under way, and how you will overcome the risks involved and provide the returns anticipated.

Why Do I Need One? A business plan will provide information on your proposed Non-Medical Home Care business to lenders, investors, and suppliers to demonstrate how you plan to use their money, and to establish a basis for credibility of your project. This plan will serve as a guide to the various areas that you as an owner will be concerned with. As you work through this plan, adapt it to your own particular needs.

Picking Your Business Name and Logo

A sure-fire way to build your business image and client confidence is through the selection of a professional business name and logo. After all, the client usually sees that FIRST before they even meet you or walk through your door.

Therefore, your business name and logo should be unique to you. Always make sure you are not mistaken with anyone else by checking with your local telephone book and county clerk's office for 'fictitious name statements'. The business name and logo should also project a definite picture in the client's mind as to what you specifically do. For instance, what denotes a more exact association? Angel Services or Angel Home Care Services?

Make an effort to be simple and direct in the choice of your name and logo. Wordy names are hard to remember and overly fancy logos can be confusing to the eye. There's a lot of room for personal and professional creativity when choosing a business name and logo, but there are three main considerations to keep in mind:

- Will your business name and logo receive trademark protection?

- Is your proposed business name and logo available?

- If your business will have a website, is a similar domain name available?

Will Your Business Name and Logo Receive Trademark Protection? Trademark law will prevent another business from using a name or logo that is likely to be confused with your business name if your business name is entitled to trademark protection. If your business is anything but a small, local business, you'll probably want to take advantage of this.

Any business name or logo used to market and identify your services is a trademark. For example, Home Instead Senior Care uses its business name to market its services. But to qualify for trademark protection under the trademark laws, your business name should be what trademark law considers "distinctive." Distinctive business names (such as Comfort Keepers, Visiting Angels, and Caring Angels) are clever and memorable, and they usually receive protection under federal and state trademark law. Common or ordinary names (such as Jones Home Care, and Tom's Senior Care) usually do not.

The best names for small businesses are those that clients can easily remember and associate with your business. For this reason, many small businesses prefer to use words that cleverly suggest qualities about the underlying product or service without describing them outright, such as Lending Tree for loans, Slenderella for diet food products, or The Body Shop for personal hygiene products. These names are also considered distinctive and are therefore protected as trademarks.

Here are a few more guidelines to use in your search for a distinctive business name:

- *Make your name memorable.* A creative, distinctive name will not only be entitled to a high level of trademark protection, but it will also stick in the minds of your clients. Forgettable names are those of people (like Williams Home Care), those that include geographic terms (like Northwest Home Care), and names that literally describe your service (like Home and Home Care, Inc.). Remember, you want to distinguish yourself from your competitors.

- *Your name should be appealing and easy to use.* Choose a name that's easy to spell and pronounce, and that is appealing to both eye and ear. Try to pick a catchy name that people will like to repeat. Make sure that any images or associations it evokes will suit your customer base.

- *Avoid geographical names.* Besides being easy to forget, and difficult to protect under trademark law, a geographical name may no longer fit if your business expands its sales or service area. If you open Jacksonville Home Care, for instance, will it be a problem if you want to open a second store in Orlando?

- *Get feedback.* Before you settle on a name, get some feedback from potential clients, suppliers and others in your support network. They may come up with a downside to a potential name or suggest an improvement you haven't thought of.

Is Your Proposed Business Name Available? Once you've come up with some ideas for distinctive names, you'll need to be sure you're not stepping on an existing name or trademark. As a first rule, don't use part of a famous name and hope you'll get away with it because you plan to use it in a different way, as in Best Buy wireless, or Dow Jones Marketing. If you attract the attention of the big guys, you'll be threatened with a lawsuit and will most likely have to change your business name on all of your marketing material.

For not so famous names, you'll have to do a name search to find out if the same name, or similar names, is already in use, and how they're being used. If another company is using the same or a similar name to market different products and services, it may be fine for you to use the name for your business. Finally, if your business is a corporation, LLC, or limited partnership, in addition to checking for existing trademarks, you must be sure your business name isn't the same as that of an existing corporation, LLC, or limited partnership in your state. You'll have to contact your state filing office to find out how to search their name databases.

Is a Domain Name Available That's Similar to Your Business Name? If your Non-Medical Home Care business will have a website, you must decide what your domain name will be. Using all or part of your business name in your domain name will make your website easier for potential clients to find. Since many domain names are already taken, check what's available before you settle on your business name. You can search for available domain names by visiting a domain name registrar such as register.com.

To do business on the Web, you'll need at least one domain name --
the .com or .net identifier that has become so familiar (and
sometimes annoying) in commercials and print advertising. You
may want to take the name you use for your business as your
domain name, with .com or .net tacked on at the end -- or you
might pick a new domain name that you think will draw people to
your website.

To help your website, and business, flourish, pick a domain name
that:

- Is easy for Web users to remember and find

- Suggests the nature of your service (Non-Medical
  Home Care)

- Serves as a strong trademark so competitors
  won't be able to use a business name or domain
  name similar to it.

- Is free of legal conflicts with trademarks belonging
  to other businesses.

Your toughest task when picking a domain name is
likely to be finding a name that's available; millions of
names have been snapped up already. For example, if
your business name is Superior Home Care, you may
find that SuperiorHomeCare.com already belongs to
someone else. In that case, you'll have to use a different
domain name (and maybe change your business name)
or pursue other options for securing the domain name
you want.

The best way to find out whether your business name is
available as a domain name is to use the search engine
at register.com or any web hosting company. Type the
name you want, select an extension to the right of the
box (which will be .com for most users), and click
"Search." You will then get a message telling you
whether or not the name is available. If it's unavailable,
scroll down to find similar names that are available.

Setting up a basic website

The first step is the actual decision to have a website developed. You will need to determine your Internet objectives and who your audience is. These essential factors will influence what type of web hosting is required.

Having an online presence for your Non-Medical Home Care business increases your visibility and professional look. Every serious business should have at least an informational site on the web.

An informational website is similar to an online business brochure. The objective of this type of site is to offer business information including the "who, what, where, when and how" of your business or organization. An informational site will allow you to show case your services to prospective clients and allow you to post company information. The process of outlining what will be contained in the site is called a website storyboard. This is essentially an outline of what pages and informational content will be included.

If you plan on hiring a staff of Web designers and programmers or have a budget to hire savvy Internet consultants, you will have a broad range of options for building a Web site. But for most small businesses with limited staff and budget resources, a turnkey solution may be more appropriate. You'll need to determine what features you need in order to choose whether this is the right approach for you. Once you've decided to go with a turnkey solution, you'll need to compare features and costs among providers. Do your homework to find a turnkey solution that's a good fit from the start to avoid unexpected fees, restrictions, and service problems that can come from making an uninformed choice. Once you've identified a prospective turnkey solution provider, you need to determine whether it can really perform. Clarify the solution's features and costs before signing up.

Ensure they have the capability to create a user-friendly website for your Non-Medical Home Care business where users can find what they're looking for quickly and efficiently. A usable website can reap huge benefits. Your website has to be easy to navigate. Users have gradually become accustomed to particular layouts and phrases on the Internet, for example:

- Organization logo is in the top-left corner and links back to the homepage

- The term 'About us' is used for organization information

- Navigation is in the same place on each page and adjacent to the content

- Anything flashing or placed above the top logo is often an advertisement

- The term 'Shopping cart' is used for items you might wish to purchase

There are numerous other conventions like these that enhance your website's usability - can you think of some more?

Don't underestimate the importance of these conventions - as the Internet matures we're getting more and more used to things being a certain way. Break these conventions and you may be left with nothing but a website with poor usability and a handful of dissatisfied site visitors.

It is essential for optimal usability that your web pages download quickly. Usability studies have shown that 8.6 seconds is the maximum time web users will wait for a page to download (source: Andrew B. King - Speed Up Your Site). The Information on your web site should be easy to retrieve. We read web pages in a different manner to the way we read printed matter. We generally don't read pages word-for-word - instead we scan. When we scan web pages certain items stand out:

- Headings

- Link text

- Bold text

- Bulleted lists

Did you notice that images were left out of that list? Contrary to the way in which we read printed matter, we see text before we see images on the Internet. For optimal website usability don't place important information in images as it might go unnoticed.

It is also important not to place restrictions on your users. Don't prevent your users from navigating through the Internet in the way that they want to. For example:

1. Every time a link is opened in a new window the back button is disabled. Approximately 60% of Web users employ the back button as their primary means of navigation If you do this then you're preventing 60% of your users from using their primary navigation - now that can't be good for usability.

2. Don't use frames to lay out your website. Frames can cause a number of usability problems, namely:

- Disabling the back button (see above)

- Bookmarking not possible

- Impossible to e-mail the link to someone else

- Problems with printing

- Users feel trapped if external links open in the same window

- Search engine optimization issues

There are lots of other ways that websites can place restrictions on its users, ultimately damaging their usability - can you think of any more? Just think back to the last time a website really infuriated you - what annoying thing did it do to make you feel that way?

An Image that Builds Your Client's Confidence in You

What's a great way to build client confidence? Project a professional image right from the very beginning. Why? Well, since the majority of individuals you will be dealing with will have high expectations, every aspect of your image needs definite attention. These include your office location and appearance, business stationery forms and cards, and even your telephone etiquette! People are basically visual. That means, what they SEE is what they think they'll get. So, build on that knowledge. Create a positive impression in the first few minutes that will garner their confidence. How?

Your staff's clothing should be clean, neat and professional. A business suit may be out of place but dirty, ragged attire is likewise. Many Non-Medical Home

Care services choose uniforms to solve this problem, but that may not be necessary if standards of good taste are followed. Your business brochures, leaflets, and proposal sheets should be organized and crisp. Tattered handouts and invoices bespeak of an I-could-care-less attitude. Secondly, people also rely on what they HEAR. You need not be an English major but speaking distinctly and slowly gains respect. Identify yourself quickly with your name and company. Tell them what you have to offer and how it can benefit them.

Better Business Tip

Have a well-developed company mission and vision

expressed around ethical values.

How can you create a positive image with the correct things to say? Don't try to be a flashy salesman with catchy phrases. Whether making calls on the telephone or in person, nothing puts off a client faster than a "wheeler dealer" impression. Honesty sells and builds confidence in a future relationship.

The Importance of Choosing Your Office Location

If you are operating on a tight budget, a home office can be an ideal solution. But, city zoning ordinances and laws may restrict this option especially if you employ on-site workers, and have clients coming and going in a never-ending stream. You must check with the community zoning department and even neighbors to avoid future misunderstandings.

For a truly professional image, though, a sign office is generally located in an office or retail area. This avoids countless problems. An office can instill a feeling of confidence the moment someone steps in the door. Not to be forgotten, too, is the FREE advertising your company receives when individuals just drive or walk by. The appearance of your office is an image-maker or image-breaker. Always show your potential clients you know what you are doing by being as organized and as tidy as possible. A sloppy and unclean office will only turn your business ship back to port. This often-overlooked aspect is one that sends a loud signal as to how clients perceive your services.

Choosing the right location for your business is important. Considerations include the needs of your services, the location of your potential clients and competitors and such things as:

- Taxes

- Zoning restrictions

- Accessibility to hospital, transit system, recreational activities and church services

- Noise

- Secure environment

It is very important to choose a layout and a design that is appropriate for clients as well as for employees. Convenience and security are two main issues to consider. To be adapted for seniors and the handicap, your office may need some of the following:

- Bath and toilet grab bars

- Handrails where needed

- Doorways which are accessible

- Good lighting

- Lever handle on doors

- Non-slip, heavy doormats and runners

4

Even if you're on the right track, you'll get run over if you just sit there.
--- Will Rogers

Getting Started!

Choosing a legal form of business

A sole proprietorship -- This is the simplest form and can be set up quickly and without much legal documentation to begin with. Make sure you procure the appropriate licenses and tax permits, keep complete business records, and at the end of the year, fill out a business tax return with your personal tax return package. That's basically all there is to it as its simplicity does hold some advantages.

A partnership -- This has some advantages, too, in that you acquire a partner to split the load of work and responsibility. But be assured, this is not as simple as it sounds. It can become a complex arrangement to draw up legal documentation through an attorney. You must spell out in advance possibilities such as: death of either party, sale of either party's share of the business, etc. In addition, you may have to take on the financial responsibilities of your partner if for some reason he or she cannot carry their load.

The day-to-day activities may bring up other issues to be dealt with such as: business direction, time each partner spends working, monetary spending, etc. At times these issues can distract from overall business sales and production.

A corporation -- This is a legal entity that operates separate from you. In other words, it owns the business and therefore is responsible for its actions, income and debts. A corporation needs legal documentation and paperwork set up through an attorney. These will be filed with the state and you must pay a state franchise tax yearly. Rates vary with each state.

Insurance: Managing Risk

Some companies operate without this last necessity: Insurance. But, a savvy business professional knows that hitting just one rock below the surface can capsize the entire ship. Liability insurance is required to keep on course in case things go wrong. Accidental injury of people and property can ruin a successful business. So, be sure you talk with a knowledgeable agent to see if you are adequately covered. Always shop around to get the best possible rate. Other areas of insurance such as health, life and retirement, deserve attention according to your needs.

Managing Your Taxes

The form of business you operate determines what taxes you must pay and how you pay them. The following are the four general types of business taxes.

- Income Tax

- Self-Employment Tax

- Employment Taxes

Income Tax
All business except partnerships must file an annual income tax return. Partnerships file an information return. The form you use depends on how your business is organized.
The federal income tax is a pay-as-you-go tax. You must pay the tax as you earn or receive income during the year. An employee usually has income tax withheld from his or her pay. If you do no pay your tax through withholding, or do not pay enough tax that way, you might have to pay estimated tax. If you are not required to make estimated tax payments, you may pay any tax due when you file your return. For additional information refer to IRS Publication 583, starting a Business and Keeping Records.

Self-Employment Tax
Self-employment tax (SE tax) is a social security and Medicare tax primarily for individuals who work for themselves. Your payments of SE tax contribute to your coverage under the social security system. Social security coverage provides you with retirement benefits, disability benefits, survivor benefits, and hospital insurance (Medicare) benefits. You must pay SE tax and file Schedule SE (Form 1040) if your net earnings from self-employment were $400 or more.
For additional information, refer to IRS Self-Employment Tax

<u>Employment Taxes</u>
If you choose to hire employees for your Non-Medical
Home Care business, you as the employer have certain
employment tax responsibilities that you must pay
and forms you must file. Employment taxes include the
following:

- Social security and Medicare taxes

- Federal income tax withholding

- Federal unemployment (FUTA) tax

For additional information, refer to IRS Employment
Taxes for Small Businesses

Determining your equipment and supplies needs

<u>Basic Home Office Essentials:</u>
A "bare bones," basic home office set-up can consist of
all or some of the following:

- Equipment: desk or flat work area; chair;
equipment needed for your specific business

- Office supplies: files, business ledger, pens,
pencils, stationery, etc.

- Telephone

- Answering machine

- Reference materials: guides, manuals, books, etc.
relevant to your business and trade.

- Computer, peripherals and business-related
software

- Fax machine

- Photocopier

- Business stationery

- Scanner

Telecoms

When getting quotes from telecommunication companies with regards to installing business telephone lines, remember to ask if a deposit is required for business. If so, ask how much per line. Phone companies have been known to quote an installation fee of about $80 per line - which sounds reasonable. There may be an initial set-up cost also. So, if you are budgeting for 3 lines, be sure you budget for the deposit and set up cost. Your organization's credit rating is used to determine whether or not a deposit is required.

Computer System

Computers are advancing so quickly that their software range can cover almost every area of your business. You need to ask yourself if you really need a computer, as they can be quite expensive (although they are getting much cheaper). Even though your Non-Medical Home Care business can probably be managed without the use of a computer, it is recommended that you purchase one. You will have a sufficient amount of paperwork, invoices, and customer databases etc that need to be completed and updated regularly. The use of a computer will give them a more professional look and can be completed with more accuracy and speed. It will also reduce the need for filing, as the data can be stored on the computer. Note: Please ensure your information is backed up regularly.

There are hundreds of different makes and models of computer, and it can be very confusing trying to find one that matches your needs and budget. The best way to find the right PC is to work out exactly what you might need it for. If it is for basic office work (E.g.: Typing letters/ invoices, basic accounts) then there is no need to buy a top or even medium specification model, as a basic 'entry-level' PC will be able to do all of these things easily.

The only reason for buying a top specification PC is if you will be using it for high-end graphics, video, and gaming (e.g.: Developing your web site with all the latest 'bells and whistles', heavy graphic design, or high quality sound and professional photographic work); and even then a basic PC will still be able to do these, just not as efficiently. Letterheads, business cards, and leaflets are more than capable of being made on most PC's from the last few years.

One feature that is worth looking for however is a CD-writer; this will allow you to make CD backups of your important data and letters in case of a future problem. They are now standard on most PC's, and they can be purchased separately for under $50 if not included (although they will need installing into the computer unit, which could void your PC's warranty).

It is possible to pick up well-priced package deals featuring fancy extras such as scanners, digital cameras, printers and web-cams. These are good if your business needs them; otherwise there is no point in getting them. Try looking out for second hand computers. They are a lot cheaper than new PC's, and even though they may not have the latest technology, they will still do all basic office work effectively.

Remember that a 5 year old PC can create letters and accounts almost as well as a brand new top of the range model. So that three year old computer you may have hidden away that is no longer suitable for games may actually be capable of fulfilling your office computer needs.

If you wish to connect your PC to a network, you will need a 'Network' connection socket. Many new PC's come with them inbuilt, but if you do not have one, you will need to buy and have installed a Network Card. Network Cards only cost between $10 and $20, but opening your PC to install it could void your PC's warranty if not carried out professionally (I.e.: Expensively!). If you wish to connect to a network, the best way is to check or ask if the PC(s) are network ready before you buy them.

Creating a working network between several PC's can be complicated depending on; the number of computers to be connected; the operating systems (E.g.: Windows XP or Windows 98); and the networking equipment you use. You should always get advice from a professional if you are unsure how to set one up properly.

<u>Software</u>
It is important that you do your homework before purchasing business software your Non-Medical Home Care Business. Business software that allows you to computerizing your accounts system will make keeping the books much easier, give your business a more professional image, improve your efficiency, and give you quick access to accurate information. There are many different reasons for using software. Routine tasks take minutes instead of days, statements and other regular correspondence can be mail-merged and personalized and up-to-date balances included. Correcting any mistakes can be done at the touch of a button and if your business is growing, a computerized accounting system will make life much easier when you take on new staff, increase your spending or have more invoices to chase.

Perhaps the most useful aspect of a computerized accounts system is the fact that once the information is recorded, it can be used to give you a snapshot of the business performance at any time, which is ideal when preparing your end of year accounts.

At the end of every financial year, your accountant will need to audit your records and, with a manual system, this can be a tedious process. If you have a computerized system, the process is made much simpler for you and your accountant. Hopefully, it will take less time to conduct the audit, and you and your staff will be free to get on with running your business

Do's and Don'ts of buying business software.

Don't

- Walk into a shop or dealership and buy the cheapest thing on offer.
  Remember, it is not the PC that does the real work, it is the software and if you buy a system that is not suited to your business it could cost you a lot of time, effort and money later on.

Do:

- Define what it is that you need your business software package to do.
  Do you want to run you whole system on it or just do some client invoicing? Will you need to automate just the main ledgers or would you like to do client tracking and client surveys on the computer? Do you have any special procedures or requirements specific to your business that you must stick to, whatever the system? It is important

that you answer these questions before you start shopping around.

- Collect some information on business software products and PCs.
  Read some of the reviews published in computer magazines.
  Talk to your accountant, who may be able to advise you about some packages. Information may also be available from authorized software dealers and large retail stores such as Staples, Best Buy etc.

Office furniture

Getting the right office furniture is very important. Having good furniture benefits your health, working practices and can even reduce the cost of employing and retaining staff. Who likes to work in a horrible environment?

Filing System- Organization may be crucial for your business so that you can find documents whenever you need them. If this is the case, then the solution is a filing cabinet. If you look around, you will be able to pick one up second hand for around $20. If not, you will be paying over $50 for a new one although small storage boxes can be purchased individually for around $5 each.

If you buy a second hand filing cabinet, you need to check whether the cabinets/drawers work properly. If there is a lock or locks, do not forget to check whether they work properly, and also if there is actually a key (and spare) for them!

Desks/Shelving- Almost everybody needs a desk in the workplace whether it is for paper work, a computer or perhaps simply for storage. Desks come in all sorts of shapes and sizes, so be sure that you find one that is most comfortable and practical for yourself and your employees.
If you buy an item such as a desk, you need to know whether it is adjustable. If an employee leaves, and a new one takes over the desk, can they adjust it (or other items such as their chair) to make it comfortable for their use?

Shelving (or storage units) will be something that you will need if your workplace is used to store information (books, magazines, discs, CDs, etc). Again, you have to consider what space you have available and nothing that is too expensive. Pinewood is always cheaper than alternative woods such as mahogany and black ash.

If you buy a desk or item of furniture second hand, remember to test whether the moving parts are working properly (E.g.: Do the drawers open, does the keyboard rack move properly. You also need to make sure that if there is a lock, that it works, and that you are given a key to it!

Chairs- When buying chairs for your employees it is important to remember that they will be using them for many hours a day. They should therefore be as comfortable and supportive as possible, with the aim of your employees keeping a healthy posture.

By paying a bit more for adjustable height chairs with arm supports and a high-back, your employees can setup their work environment to be comfortable, and therefore be more productive. This is especially important when your employees are using computers, and may be sat in the same area for long periods of time.

Office chairs cost from under $30 to well over $200, depending on the size, material, adjustability and features. Simple desks can be found for under $100 and can stretch up to $300 for something that offers more facilities, space and perhaps more style. Know how much space you have in your workplace or things could get too crowded and impractical if you buy something too big, one large desk may be ok, but three large desks in a small office could seriously affect the quality of the working conditions.

Is the furniture you buy comfortable? Remember that either you or your employees will be using the furniture for many hours a day; something stylish but uncomfortable or oddly shaped can affect the comfort and productivity of your workers.

It is vital to know whether an employee's desk is right for them. Is it at the right height to allow comfortable work; are there drawers or keyboard racks that affect the space available for using the desk? If you are in doubt then either take the person who will be using the desk to test it, or get an idea of the space and height they need to use it before buying.

If you have bought a PC and a desk to use together, are you certain that they will fit the spaces you expect? There are many different types and sizes of PC, and many different types of desks, by measuring the spaces you intend to fill, you can be sure that your purchases will work together effectively.

What Licenses and permits are required?

Your Non-Medical Home Care business will probably have to be licensed through your state and/or local municipality. Some states may require your Non-Medical Home Care employees be licensed also. Licensing requirements will depend upon your business services. Typically Non-medical Home Care has fewer requirements than Medical Home Care. Before you open your doors, be sure to go to your County Courthouse and find out if you need to get a business license. You will also find out if the area from which you plan to operate your business is zoned for your type of business. Normally, the person you talk to at the Courthouse will also be able to give you advice regarding a Taxpayers Identification Number or a Federal Identification Number, which are generally filed by you with the Secretary of State's office in your state.

DIY *vs. Hiring professional services: Accountants, Attorneys etc.*

The use of professional services is essential to the success of a small business. Since Non-Medical Home Care service comprises many disciplines, professionals can provide knowledge and expertise in the areas where you may have little. They can round out your management team to ensure your business is operating efficiently. Under no circumstances should you attempt to render professional services that you are not qualified for, such as nursing, social work and legal advice.

As an entrepreneur, there are professionals which you t or mig e a perso ese may

- Lawyer
- Social worker
- Dietitian
- Doctor
- Nurse
- Physiothera pist

- Occupational therapist in
- Pharmacist
- Ambulance driver
- Insurance broker
- Accountant
- Banker

The use of professional services is essential to the success of a small business. Professionals can provide knowledge and expertise in areas where you may have little. They can also round out your management team to ensure that your business is operating efficiently.

As an entrepreneur, there are four main areas of professional services that you may wish to consult:

accountant, lawyer, banker and insurance broker.

When seeking out professional help, choose carefully.
Find someone with whom you feel you can establish a
good working relationship. When searching for names,
ask family members, friends, and businesses associates
as well as consulting the business pages in your
telephone book.

For first time meetings, be prepared to explain your
situation and what you are looking for. Ask what
services the firm provides and how it can assist you. Do
not forget to ask how much the firm charges for its
services.

Selecting an Accountant

Accountants are highly trained professionals who deal
with business records, financial matters, and other
aspects of planning and running a business.
Accountants can:

- Help you put a business plan together and
  provide financial advice;

- Advise you on the form of business organization
  that is best for you;

- Do your bookkeeping and/or provide bookkeeping
  training;

- Prepare your financial statements and explain
  them;

- Prepare corporate and income tax returns and
  other information required by government.

Hourly fees may vary depending on the kind of work, complexity of the work and the accountant's professional experience.

If you need someone to simply keep your financial books updated, you may want to consider hiring a bookkeeper. This may be a less expensive alternative.

Selecting a Lawyer

Lawyers are highly trained professionals who deal with a full range of personal and business legal matters. Lawyers tend to specialize in one or more areas of practice.

If your legal concerns are restricted to one specific area, it may be best for you to deal with a lawyer who specializes in that area. Many business transactions have legal implications, so you should try to find a lawyer who you can treat as a trusted business advisor.

Some advice that lawyers can provide involve:

- Help in choosing the correct legal form that is right for your business venture;

- Help in drawing up the documentation for the business;

- Help in understanding and observing zoning laws and local legal requirements;

- Aid in conforming with government regulation and record keeping;

- Help in developing contracts with landlords, suppliers, clients, etc.;

- Help in understanding and arranging leases. Hourly fees or charges vary widely from lawyer to lawyer, depending on the complexity of the issues, the services required, and the degree of experience of the lawyer.

Selecting a Banker

Your commercial banking relationship is a matter that requires careful selection and the foundation for a long-term commitment. Changing banks is far more difficult and expensive with a business account than with a personal account because commercial services are more customized and time consuming to negotiate.

Many of the reasons why individuals select a bank for personal needs are just as valid for business needs. You must consider price, quality, attitude, reputation, service, convenience, safety, and reliability.

These are a few critical factors that a business manager should bear in mind when selecting a banker.

Attitude toward your business - Are they interested in your problems? Are they active in the community? Are they interested in creating a relationship?

Credit services - Does the branch provide operating loans, term loans, letters of credit, guarantees, franchise financing, leasing, and government guaranteed loans?

Size and management policies of the bank - Will your maximum requirements fall within their limit? How concerned is the banker with the growth and prosperity of your community?

- *Cash management service* - How does the bank's portfolio of services meet your needs? Services to consider: automated payrolls, payment distribution, transfer of funds, lock boxes, and 24-hour depository services.

A preliminary meeting with potential lenders is a good idea. You can outline your general plans and learn the needs of the lending institution and its services. To establish a good rapport with the lender, it is important to create confidence in your ability. Plan your project in advance and give the lender time to consider your business plan.

Banks generally will not lend you 100% of your start up financing. Your bank is a lender, not an owner or shareholder of your business. The bank will request that you invest some of your own money as a symbol of your commitment.

Selecting an Insurance Agent

Insurance is an essential part of financial planning. Unless you are willing to pay personally for business catastrophes and lawsuits, you will need to consult an insurance agent and purchase insurance.

You may not be aware of the types of business catastrophes that could conceivably occur in your business. It is the job of your insurance agent to tailor a policy that best fits your needs. Here are some examples of insurance coverage that would protect you against a claim.

Personal liability - protects against claims made by those who suffer bodily injury on your premises.

Product liability - protects against lawsuits by clients who are injured while using your services.

Fire - will enable you to rebuild or repair the business location as well as replace equipment and inventory in the event of fire damage.

Automobile - protects your vehicle during business use.

Disability - will provide income during a period when you cannot work.

Business interruption - compensates for lost earnings during a temporary halt in business caused by a major disaster such as fire, tornado, flood, etc.

Life - provides protection against financial loss caused by your death or serious injury.

Workers' Compensation - covers treatment of injuries and loss of pay related to employee accidents or illness on the job.

Crime/Theft - reimburses for losses due to robbery, burglary, and employee dishonesty.

Bonding - ensures protection for faithful representation.

Financial Management & Budgeting

Are you going to be in control of your new business? Will you know in advance about any looming cash flow problems? Unless you use properly prepared budgets, the answer is probably going to be no. Budgeting sets out the financial targets for your business. It helps you anticipate problems and compare what has actually happened with what you expected.

At this point, take some time to think about what it will take to get your Non-Medical Home Care business up and running. This section is designed to help you layout you financial management plan starting with identify your start up cost.

The first question concerns the source of your start up dollars. After your initial capital investment, the major source of money is the sale of your services. What dollar volume of business do you expect to do in the next 12 months?

In connection with your annual dollar volume of business, you need to think about expenses. If, for example you plan to do $100,000 in business, what will it cost you to do this amount of servicing? And even more important, what will be left over as profit at the end of the year? Never lose sight of the fact that profit is your pay. Even if you pay yourself a salary for living expenses, your business must make a profit if it is to continue year after year and pay back the money you invested in it.

It's critical to determine how much cash you'll need to open and operate your Non-Medical Home Care business before you hang out your shingle. To keep your business running smoothly in its startup phase, you'll need enough capital to cover all expenses until you reach the break-even point. Many experts recommend new companies start out with enough money to cover projected expenses for at least six months. It's foolhardy to expect to generate revenue immediately—it's best to play it safe and plan for all contingencies. As for determining accurate cost estimates, a good rule of thumb is to assume everything will cost more than you expect, so pad your numbers in order to create a safety net. Tally and double-check the numbers before you begin writing your business plan and searching for startup funds.

<u>Start-up Costs</u>
If you are starting a new Non-Medical Home Care
business, list the following estimated start-up costs:

Furniture and equipment	$ __________
Labor Cost	$ __________
Supplies	$ __________
Decorating and remodelling	$ __________
Signage	$ __________
Deposit for utilities	$ __________
Rent	$ __________
Legal and professional fees	$ __________
Insurance	$ __________
Taxes	$ __________
Licenses and permits	$ __________
Advertising for opening	$ __________
Operating cash	$ __________
Other expenses	$ __________
Total	$ __________

Whether you have the funds to start your Non-Medical Home Care business or borrow them, your new business will have to pay back these start-up costs. Keep this fact in mind as you work on the financial aspects of your Business. The quick estimate of expenses above provides a starting point. The next step is to break down your expenses so they can be handled over the next 12 months. A budget helps you to see the dollar amount of your expenses each month. Then from month to month the question is: Will sales bring in enough money to pay your bills on time? The answer is "yes" if you do your homework by preparing for the peaks and valleys that are in many Non-Medical Home Care service operations. A cash forecast is a management tool that can eliminate much of the anxiety that can plague you if your business goes through lean months. Suppose at this point you have determined that your business needs more money than can be generated by sales. What do you do? What you do depends on the situation. For example, the need may be for bank credit to tide your business over during the lean months. This loan can be repaid during the fat sales months when expenses are far less than sales. Adequate working capital is necessary for success and survival. Whether you seek to borrow money for only a month or so or on a long-term basis, the lender needs to know whether or not your business financial position is strong or weak. Your lender will ask to see a current cash forecast. Even if you don't need to borrow, it is recommended that you draw up a cash forecast of your business financial condition. Moreover, if you don't need to borrow money, you may want to show your plan to the bank that handles your business checking account. It is never too early to build good relations with your banker, to show that you are a manager who knows where you want to go rather than a business owner who hopes to make a success. The cash forecast sets out your expected turnover for each month of the next year.

Base your expected volume of sales from the services and the prices you intend to charge.

The following are questions you should consider when preparing your budget.

- If you have previous experience in the Non-Medical Home Care industry, what was the month-by-month pattern of sales figures in past years?
- Will the sales pattern be the same in your new business?
- What sales are you confident of achieving?
- Do you have any firm contracts with clients?
- Will there be regular clients you can rely on?
- Do you have the capacity to meet increasing demand as your business grows?
- What impact will your marketing have?
- What effect will any price changes have on sales volumes?
- What is your competition doing?
- Are you expecting to take clients from your competitors?
- How is the economic climate changing?
- In recent months have the Non-Medical Home Care industry's sales in your area been higher or lower than a year ago?
- Do you expect any special circumstances to have an effect on your sales? For example, local events.
- What does the completed sales budget show? Do the monthly figures look realistic?

Balance Sheet

The Balance Sheet is a statement detailing what a company owns (assets) and claims against the company (liabilities and owners' equity) on a particular date. Some people describe the balance sheet as a snapshot of a company's financial health. A balance sheet comprises assets, liabilities, and owners' or stockholders' equity. Assets and liabilities are divided into short- and long-term obligations including cash accounts such as checking, money market, or government securities. At any given time, assets must equal liabilities plus owners' equity. An asset is anything the business owns that has monetary value. Liabilities are the claims of creditors against the assets of the business.

ASSETS = LIABILITIES + OWNERS' EQUITY

What is a balance sheet used for? A balance sheet helps a small business owner quickly get a handle on the financial strength and capabilities of the business. Is the business in a position to expand? Can the business easily handle the normal financial ebbs and flows of revenues and expenses? Or should the business take immediate steps to bolster cash reserves?

Balance sheets can identify and analyze trends, particularly in the area of receivables and payables. Is the receivables cycle lengthening? Can receivables be collected more aggressively? Is some debt uncollectible? Has the business been slowing down payables to forestall an inevitable cash shortage?

Better Business Tip

Paying payables electronically can provide you with additional control over your accounts payable. Instead of having to write and mail in a check, you can set up an electronic funds transfer from your business checking account to the parties you need to pay.

Balance sheets are one of the most basic elements in providing financial reporting to potential lenders such as banks, investors, and vendors who are considering how much credit to grant the firm.

Jo Ann's Home Care Services
Balance Sheet
December 31, 2005

ASSETS
Current Assets:

Cash	35,000	
Account Receivable	40,000	
Total Current Assets		75,000

Non-Current Assets

Fixed Assets	80,000	
Less Accumulated Depreciation	(15,000)	
Fixed Assets (net)	65,000	
Advances to Owners	5,000	
Total Non-Current Assets		70,000

Total Assets (35 + 70)		**145,000**

LIABILITIES

Current Liabilities

Current Portion of Long-Term Debt	5,000	
Note Payable	20,000	
Accrued Taxes		
Account Payable (A/P)	15,000	
Total Current Liabilities		42,000

Long-Term Liabilities

Loan Payable	21,000	
Total Long-Term Liabilities		21,000
Total Liabilities (42 + 21)		

CAPITAL OR NET WORTH

Owners Investment	25,000	
Retained Earnings	57,000	
Total Capital (Net worth)		82,000

Total Liabilities & Capital (63 + 82)		**145,000**

<u>Income Statement</u>
An income statement, otherwise known as a profit and loss statement, is a summary of a company's profit or loss during any one given period of time, such as a month, three months, or one year. The income statement records all revenues for a business during this given period, as well as the operating expenses for the business.

What are income statements used for? You use an income statement to track revenues and expenses so that you can determine the operating performance of your business over a period of time. Small business owners use these statements to find out what areas of their business are over budget or under budget. Specific items that are causing unexpected expenditures can be pinpointed, such as phone, fax, mail, or supply expenses. Income statements can also track dramatic increases in cost of goods sold as a percentage of sales. They also can be used to determine income tax liability.

Income statements are one of the most basic elements required by potential lenders, such as banks, investors, and vendors. They will use the financial reporting contained therein to determine credit limits.

Jo Ann's Home Care Services
INCOME STATEMENT
December 31, 2005
SALES

Net Sales	$300,000
Cost of Sales	$80,000
GROSS PROFIT (300 less 80)	$220,000

OPERATING EXPENSES

Advertising/Promotion	$3,000
Public Relations	$2,500
Travel	$7,500
Miscellaneous	$500
Payroll	$90,000
Lease Equipment	$6,000
Utilities	$7,500
Insurance	$3,600
Rent	$18,000
Professional Services	$4,400
Total Operating Expenses	$143,000
Operating Income (220 less 143)	$77,000
Interest Expense	$10,000

PROFIT

Net Profit before taxes (77 less 10)	$67,000
Less: All Income Taxes	$22,000
Net Profit (67 less 22)	**$45,000**

Cash Flow Statement

The Cash Flow Statement details the exchange of cash between your business and the outside world. The flow is categorized as:

- Flow "in" from Operations
  (cash the company made by selling services)

- Flow "in" from Financing
  (cash the company raised by loans, grants etc.)

- Flow "out" to Investing
  (cash the company spent investing in its future growth)

Each of these flows can actually flow both ways. Investors like to see that the company can cover its spending with cash from operations, without having to turn to financing.

The cash flow statement also has to reconcile the net effect of these flows with the difference in its cash holdings at the beginning and end dates of the reporting period.

Where the Balance Sheet and the Profit and Loss account are primarily prepared for your 'actual' year end figures for submission to Companies House, the Cash Flow Forecast needs to be, some say, pessimistic as to your sales figure and expenses. One problem we all face at some stage is preparation of a Cash Flow Forecast for the bank manager. It is 'almost' impossible to submit honest figures when you use pessimistic figures - when you look at the finished result you say to yourself 'I would not give anyone a loan if I saw these figures'.

However, I suggest you do use pessimistic figures and inform the lender that the figures are pessimistic, and as such, are very achievable. Returning to your lender 6 - 12 months after arranging a loan or overdraft facility, and asking for more funding because your original figures were way out, will not impress the lender.

The example below evenly spreads out all costs. In reality, utilities, lease, etc. can be paid quarterly, some in advance, others in arrears. It is advisable to enter the proper amount in the month that the payment is due to ensure you are aware of the highs and lows of your cash requirements. However, the example below is a good tool for setting out your budget.

In most cases, a business should forecast for a 12-month period. However, we have cut our example down to 3-months...just so that you get the idea. In addition, we have simplified the content (listings on the left-hand-side) to make it easier to follow and understand.

All figures in $	Open	Jan	Feb	March
INCOME				
Sales		20,000	23,000	25,000
Capital In	25,000			
TOTAL INCOME	**25,000**	**20,000**	**27,000**	**30,000**
FINANCES / ASSETS				
Loan Repayments		500	500	500
Interest Paid		50	50	50
TOTAL FINANCES / ASSETS		**550**	**550**	**550**
DIRECT COSTS				
Cost of Sales		6,000	7,000	5,000
TOTAL DIRECT COSTS		**6,000**	**7,000**	**5,000**
EXPENSES				
Salary		8,000	15,000	15,000
Office Rent		800	800	800
Telephone		125	150	100
Utilities		175	200	125
Insurance		350	350	350
TOTAL EXPENSES		**9,450**	**16,500**	**16,375**
OPENING BALANCE*	-	10,000	14,000	16,950
TOTAL INCOME	10,000	20,000	27,000	30,000
TOTAL OUTGOINGS	-	16,000	24,050	21,925
NET CASH FLOW*	10,000	4,000	2,950	8,075
ENDING BALANCE*	10,000	14,000	16,950	**25,025**

* Negative figures would be denoted by (parenthesis) i.e. (500)

The last five rows of the forecast are:

Opening Balance - This figure is the ending balance of the previous month

Total Income - This is the total income figure for the month (highlighted in blue).

Total Outgoings - This is the combined total of the outgoings (highlighted in yellow). In this case, we have three outgoing costs for each month (finance, direct costs and expenses).

Net Cash Flow - This is the difference between the total income and the total outgoings. It is worked out by subtracting the total outgoings from the total income.

Ending Balance - This is the ending balance at the end of the month. This figure is obtained by adding (or subtracting if it is a negative net cash flow) the net cash flow to the opening balance of the month.

RATIO ANALYSIS

The Balance Sheet and the Statement of Income are essential, but they are only the starting point for successful financial management. Apply Ratio Analysis to Financial Statements to analyze the success, failure, and progress of your business.

Ratio Analysis enables you to spot trends in your business and to compare its performance and condition with the average performance of similar businesses in the same industry. To do this compare your ratios with the average of businesses similar to yours and compare your own ratios for several successive years, watching especially for any unfavorable trends that may be starting. Ratio analysis may provide the all-important early warning indications that allow you to solve your business problems before they destroy your business.

These Liquidity, Leverage, Profitability, and Management Ratios will allow you to identify trends in your business and compare its progress with the performance of others through data published by various sources. Thus allowing you to determine the your business's relative strengths and weaknesses. Important Balance Sheet Ratios measure liquidity and solvency (a business's ability to pay its bills as they come due) and leverage (the extent to which the business is dependent on creditors' funding). Liquidity Ratios indicate the ease of turning assets into cash. They include the Current Ratio and Working Capital.

<u>Liquidity Ratios</u>

Current Ratio - The current ratio measures your company's capacity to pay its debts as they come due. The current ratio is the ratio between all current assets and all current liabilities, another way of expressing liquidity. 1:1 current ratio means; the company has $1.00 in current assets to cover each $1.00 in current liabilities. Your business should strive for a current ratio above 1:1 and as close to 2:1 as possible. One problem with the current ratio is that it ignores timing of cash received and paid out. Thus, the current ratio tells very little about the company's ability to survive

Number Source: Balance Sheet page 63

<table>
<tr><td colspan="3">F O R M U L A</td></tr>
<tr><td>Current Assets</td><td>$75,000</td><td rowspan="2">= 1.79</td></tr>
<tr><td>Current Liabilities</td><td>$42,000</td></tr>
</table>

If you feel your business's current ratio is too low, you may be able to raise it by:

- Paying some debts.

- Increasing your current assets from loans or other borrowings with a maturity of more than one year.

- Converting non-current assets into current assets.

- Increasing your current assets from new equity contributions.

- Putting profits back into the business.

Working Capital - The formula for working capital is current assets minus current liabilities. Working capital measures how much in liquid assets your company has available to build its business. The number can be positive or negative; depending on how much debt the company is carrying. In general, companies that have a lot of working capital will be more successful since they can expand and improve their operations. Companies with negative working capital may lack the funds necessary for growth.

Number Source: Balance Sheet page 63

F O R M U L A	
Current Assets	$75,000
Current Liabilities	- $42,000
	$33,000

Leverage Ratio - This Leverage Ratio indicates the extent to which your business is reliant on debt financing (creditor money versus owner's equity). Generally, the higher this ratio, the more risky a creditor will perceive its exposure in your business, making it correspondingly harder to obtain credit.

Number Source: Balance Sheet (page 63)

<table>
<tr><td colspan="3">F O R M U L A</td></tr>
<tr><td>Total Liabilities
Total Net Worth</td><td>$63,000
$82,000</td><td>=   .77</td></tr>
</table>

Profitability Ratio Analysis

Profitability Ratios measures your Business's profitability. They include Gross Margin Ratio and Net Profit Margin Ratio.

Gross Margin Ratio - This ratio is the percentage of sales dollars left after subtracting the cost of sales from net sales. It measures the percentage of sales dollars available to pay the overhead expenses of the company.

Comparison of your business ratios to those of similar businesses will reveal the relative strengths or weaknesses in your business. The Gross Margin Ratio is calculated as follows:

Number Source: Income Statement page 65

<table>
<tr><td colspan="3">F O R M U L A</td></tr>
<tr><td>Gross Profit
Net Sales</td><td>$220,000
$300,000</td><td>=   .73</td></tr>
</table>

Reminder: Gross Profit = Net Sales - Cost of Goods Sold

Net Profit Margin Ratio - This ratio is the percentage of sales dollars left after subtracting the Cost of Sales and all expenses, except income taxes. It provides a good opportunity to compare your company's "return on sales" with the performance of other companies in your industry. It is calculated before income tax because tax rates and tax liabilities vary from company to company for a wide variety of reasons, making comparisons after taxes much more difficult. The Net Profit Margin Ratio is calculated as follows:

Number Source: Income Statement page 65

<table>
<tr><td colspan="2">F O R M U L A</td></tr>
<tr><td>Net Profit before Tax
$67,000
────────────   =   .22
Net Sales
$300,000</td></tr>
</table>

Management Ratios

Other important ratios, often referred to as Management Ratios, are also derived from Balance Sheet and Statement of Income information. They include Accounts Receivable Turnover Ratio, Return on Assets Ratio, and Return on Investment Ratio.

Accounts Receivable Turnover Ratio - This ratio indicates how well accounts receivable are being collected. If receivables are not collected reasonably in accordance with their terms, you should rethink your collection policy. If receivables are excessively slow in being converted to cash, liquidity could be severely impaired.

Number Source: Balance Sheet (page 63) and Income Statement (page 65)

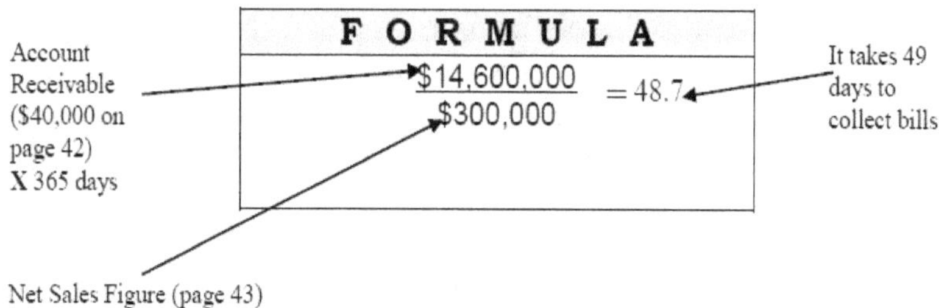

Return on Assets Ratio - This measures how efficiently profits are being generated from the assets employed in your business when compared with the ratios of firms in a similar business. A low ratio in comparison with industry averages indicates an inefficient use of business assets. The Return on Assets Ratio is calculated as follows:

Number Source: Balance Sheet (page 63) and Income Statement (page 65)

FORMULA		
Net Profit before Tax	$67,000	= .46
Total Assets	$145,000	

Return on Investment (ROI) Ratio - The ROI is perhaps the most important ratio of all. It is the percentage of return on funds invested in the business by its owners. In short, this ratio tells the owner whether or not all the effort put into the business has been worthwhile. If the ROI is less than the rate of return on an alternative, risk-free investment such as a bank savings account, the owner may be wiser to sell the company, put the money in such a savings instrument, and avoid the daily struggles of small business management. The ROI is calculated as follows:

Number Source: Balance Sheet (page 63) and Income Statement (page 65)

<table>
<tr><td colspan="3">F O R M U L A</td></tr>
<tr><td>Net Profit before Tax
Net Worth</td><td>$67,000
$82,000</td><td>= .82</td></tr>
</table>

Profits! Profits! Profits!

Profit can be defined simply as revenues - expenses = profit. So, to increase profits, you must raise revenues, lower expenses or both. Making a profit is the most important -- some might say the only objective of a business. Profit measures success.

<u>Sufficiency of Profit</u>
The following questions are designed to help you measure the adequacy of the profit your business is making. Making a profit is only the first step; making enough profit to survive and grow is really what business is all about.

- Have you compared your profit with your profit goals?

- Is it possible your goals are too high or too low?

- Have you compared your present profits with the profits made in the last one to three years?

- Have you compared your profits with profits made by similar firms in your line?

A number of organizations publish financial ratios for various businesses, among them Robert Morris Associates and Dun and Bradstreet. Remember, these published ratios are only averages. You probably want to be better than average.

Have you analyzed the direction your profits have been taking? The preceding analyzes, with all their merits, report on a firm only at a single time in the past. It is not possible to use these isolated moments to indicate the trend of your business performance. To do a trend analysis performance indicator absolute amounts or ratios should be computed for several time periods (monthly for several months, for example) and the results laid out in columns side by side for easy comparison, you can then evaluate your performance, see the direction it's taking, and make initial forecasts of where it will go.

Does your firm provide several distinct Non-Medical Home Care services? If it does, a separate profit and ratio analysis of each should be made:

- To show the relative contribution by each service;

- To show the relative burden of expenses by each service;

- To show which items are most profitable, which are less so, and which are losing money.

- To show which are slow and fast moving.

The profit and ratio analyses of each major item help you find out the strong and weak areas of your operations. They can help you make profit-increasing decisions to drop services or to place particular emphasis behind one or another.

Developing Your Business Plan

The first and most important step towards starting your Non-Medical Home Care business is to develop a detailed business plan. Don't overlook this vital part of starting your business. It will save you time, money and energy in the future. This plan should be carefully thought-out and written down. It should include all of your plans and goals for your business -- financial, personal, location, etc. -- and the steps that you need to take to implement those plans.

Better Business Tip

Get an advisory board or a mentor. This may sound crazy for a small operation, but it's really not. Ask family members or friends whom you trust to be your board of directors. They should review your business plans and results regularly. Having someone to give you an objective opinion is critical.

In order to qualify for a loan to finance your Non-Medical Home Care business, you will need to write a business plan or proposal. Any lender or grantor will want to know the reasons why they should give or lend you money, thus, they will need to see a business plan. It not only outlines business strategies, planning and forecasting, but it's also an exercise to help you focus on where business is headed. It forces you to crystallize opportunities and challenges and make plans to meet objectives and provide for possible contingencies.

In addition, your newly completed business plan can be used as the foundation for a loan proposal to your local banker. Your business plan should be attached to a one-page cover letter that summarizes your loan request. Address this cover letter to your loan officer and briefly cover the five following points:

1. Purpose of loan

2. Amount required

3. Term of loan

4. Source of repayment (remember the 4 Cs?)

5. Collateral available (again, the 4 Cs)

If you feel your finance or accounting knowledge is not sufficient to prepare these statements, seek professional assistance. There are agencies that will help you with writing your business plan for free. Check with your local or regional Small Business Development Center. Another agency that provides free assistant is SCORE. SCORE stands for Service Corps of Retired Executives. SCORE's 10,500 volunteers provide small business counseling and training through a network of 389 chapters, 800 branches and its Web site www.score.org. SCORE is a resource partner with the U.S. Small Business Administration. SCORE has served more than 7 million entrepreneurs since 1964. In fiscal year 2004, SCORE volunteers spent 1.42 million hours helping entrepreneurs.

Your business financing must be planned meticulously to insure success. The business plan is your company's principle sales tool in raising money. Before risking any capital, investors want to assure themselves that you have thought through your plans carefully, that you know what you are doing, and that you can respond effectively to problems and opportunities. They will insist on seeing your business plan before considering any investment, and often will not even meet with you without prior review of it. A well-written business plan serves as a communication tool, conveying the potential of your company. It should address all major issues, yet not be so detailed that it "turns off" the investor/reader. Your business plan must paint a picture for the reader and speak for you in your absence.

Below is an overall outline of a business plan. Each area includes a brief description of what information you need to include. By following these guidelines, you should be well on your way to writing a comprehensive and successful business plan.

I. Introduction/Summary

This is the most crucial part of your plan. You will want to capture the readers' interest right from the very beginning. Summarize the what, where, why, how, etc. of your business. The purpose of this section is to give the investor some context in which to fit all that you are about to say concerning your services and the Non-Medical Home Care market.

This overview should include the following information:

A. Name and location of business

B. Legal structure (Sole Proprietor, Partnership, Subchapter S or C Corporation)

C. Principal owners (full names)

D. Definition of business

    1. Type (Non-Medical Home Care service)

    2. Is this a new start, expansion, or acquisition?

E. History of the business

F. State why this business should exist

1. Motivation of the entrepreneur

2. Benefit to the community or industry

G. Major obstacles

H. Major strengths

<u>II. Services</u>
The purpose of this section is to give the investor some context in which to fit all that you are about to say concerning your Non-Medical Home Care services and its market. This area should clearly present the business that you are in, the services you will offer, the nature of your industry and the opportunities to market your services. Also include here the difference between your competitors and your company's offerings. The description of your services should be technically accurate, including the standard industrial classification (SIC) code for financial proposals.

<u>III. Operations Plan</u>
This section should describe the location, physical facility, space requirements, major equipment, labor force, sources of supply, layout and floor plan that are required to provide your service. This portion of the Business Plan should also explain your business would be managed on a day-to-day basis. Insurance, lease or rent agreements and other issues pertinent to your business will be included here as necessary. The outline below covers the major areas of the Operations Plan section:

A. Location

1. Does the location have an impact on your ability to reach clients?

2. What are the physical characteristics of the current or proposed location? (What improvements are necessary?)

B. Physical facility (discuss existing status and required changes)

1. Vehicle access for clients and suppliers

2. Inventory storage

3. Equipment, fixtures, and furniture

4. Electricity, heat, air conditioning, venting, wastewater

5. Compliance with current and future regulations and other legislation

6. Capability for expansion

C. Labor

1. What skills and experience are required?

IV. Market Analysis

The purpose of this section of the plan is to present enough facts to convince the investor that your Non-Medical Home Care service has a substantial market in a growing industry and can achieve sales despite the competition. Although this area is one of the most difficult to prepare, it is also one of the most important. Many of the subsequent sections of the business plan depend on sales estimates that are developed here. The sales levels you project based on market research and analysis directly influence the size of your operation, the marketing plan and the amount of debt and equity capital you will require.

Keep in mind; to generate a consistent and increasing sales flow, you must become knowledgeable about your market - the people that might buy your service.

Included here as well is information on your competition and how you will differentiate your service from others like it. When putting this information together, thoroughly research so you can provide proof of a demand for your services. Take time to do this section very well. Check alternate sources for market date for key numbers such as market size and growth rates. The outline here provides a guide for preparing the Market Analysis portion of your business plan.

A. Industry trends

   1. Projections/trends for the Non-Medical Home Care industry.

   2. At what stage of the service life cycle would your business be entering the market? (Introduction, growth, maturity, saturation, or decline)

B. Description of total market
   One way to define the total market is to use important characteristics from the census, local Chambers of Commerce, the public library, trade associations, etc.

   1. What is the present size of the entire market?

   2. What is your market's growth potential?

   3. Discuss the economic, social, demographic, and political characteristics of this market and the impact on your business.

C. Target market.
   The target market is that segment of the total market that is likely potential clients. A clear understanding of the demographics; geographic location, age, income, education, sex, etc. and psychographics; likes, dislikes, and tendencies that affect purchasing patterns can help you develop a strategy to reach the target market through your sales plan.

1. What is the size of your target market?

2. What percentage of the target market do you anticipate?

3. How will you attract and keep this market?

4. How can you expand your market?

D. Documentation of demand for your service. Although personal experience is certainly a good basis for your assumptions, you must also provide proof from a third party to add credibility.

1. Published statistics (industry association, trade journal, news articles)

2. Primary market survey (data you gathered or paid for from a professional market research firm)

3. Contracts, letters of commitment, letters of interest

E. Competition

1. Who are they?

2. Where are they located?

3. How do they compare to your business?

a. Sales volume

b. Number of employees

c. Number of locations

d. Number of clients

4. Is their business steady, increasing, or decreasing?

5. What are your competitor's strengths and weaknesses?

6. Does your competition extend credit?

7. What have you learned by observing them?

F. Service differentiation

1. What unique niche of the market will this business fill?

a. Has anyone attempted to fill this niche? If not, why?

b. Are there a patent, trademark, copyright, or trade secret that will give you a head start on the competition?

c. Where do you believe you have a business advantage? (Price, services, customer service, other)

V. Sales Strategy

The sales strategy of your business plan covers a wide variety of areas, but should clearly explain how your service will be priced and promoted. Your pricing policy is one of the more important decisions you will have to make. Be sure not to get caught in the trap of offering a "superior service for a lower price." By offering a price that is too low, you may be sending a message that your service is either not as good as you say it is, therefore you must offer it at a lesser cost. Starting too low can make it difficult to raise prices - it is much easier to cut prices. Also, don't underestimate the costs of running your business. Proper pricing will ensure you have enough money to provide your services, make a profit and continue to grow in order to remain competitive. Now that you have conquered pricing, you will need to get the message out! Your promotional efforts must be well-planned, researched and properly executed in order to see results that will justify the costs of advertising and the time needed to personally sell your service. Finally, be sure to include information on how conveniences will further promote the sale of your service. Taking the time to consider the "little things" can go a long way in attracting and retaining a solid client base. The outline below will guide you in putting together your sales strategy.

   A. Pricing policy

       1. What is the relationship between the price you will charge and the image of the business you are trying to create?

       2. How will you price?

   B. Promotional efforts.
Make sure your cash flow reflects monies budgeted for these activities and the image/position you are attempting to establish match your promotional activities.

       1. Advertising

          a. Direct mail

          b. Store sign

          c. Radio and television

          d. Magazines, newspapers, and trade journals

          e. Outdoor sign, poster

          f. Trade shows

g. Novelties (calendars, pencils, magnets, etc.)

h. Yellow pages

2. Personal selling.
   Every promotional effort is an expense of time or money. The advertising tools listed above involve substantial expenditures of money. How can /does this apply to you?

   a. Customer service

   b. Knowledgeable staff

   c. Complimentary products/services

   d. Community involvement

3. Publicity (free advertising)

   a. Press release (newspapers, radio and television news stations cover stories of interest to their audience: unique offerings, interesting and special events.)

VI. Management Plan

The management team is the key to turning a good idea into a successful business. Investors look for a committed management team with a balance of technical, managerial and business skills, and the experience in doing what is proposed. This section of the business plan will be of primary interest to potential investors and will significantly influence their investment decisions. It should include a description of the key management personnel and their primary duties, as well as the organizational structure of the company's main participants. The outline here explains each section of this area. This section should include the personal history of the principals, related work experience, duties and responsibilities, salaries, organizational chart, and resources available to the business.

A. Personal history of key participants (complete this section for each key participant in the business)

1. Business background

2. Management experience

3. Education (formal and informal learning experiences)

4. Personal data

   a. Full name and spouse's full name

   b. Present address

   c. Social security number

   d. Driver's license number

5. Relate past experience to future success potential (Include letter of recommendation, if possible)

B. Duties and responsibilities of key participants

1. Organizational chart (Who are the decision makers? Is there appropriate delegation of authority and tasks?)

2. Job descriptions

C. Compensation

1. Salaries, hourly rates

2. Other incentives

D. Available resources
Do you have the marketing, management, and financial skills to do it all yourself? If not, then show relationships that fill the gaps to create a fully capable business enterprise. Even if you do, do you network with others in your industry to stay current on changes in the marketplace?

1. Professional (Lawyer, CPA)

2. Insurance

3. Consultants

4. Associations (Chamber of Commerce, Professional or Trade groups)

VII. Financial Analysis

The financial plan is basic to the evaluation of an investment opportunity and should represent your best estimates of future operations. Its purpose is to indicate your venture's potential and the timetable for financial viability. It can also serve as an operating plan for financial management of the venture.

This portion of your business plan should include actual exhibits of estimated statements. You will be describing the needed sources for your funds and the uses you intend for the money you receive. Here a budget will be included, naturally, but also numbers explaining start-up costs, projected monthly cash flow, equipment needed, and personal financial information. The outline here takes these items into consideration and provides a guide for beginning work on your own financial analysis.

A. Startup Costs

1. How much will it cost you to open your doors?

2. Allow enough working capital for expenses during the early period.

B. Source and use of funds

1. Of the total money you've identified for starting the business, how much are you contributing, and how much comes from the financial institution or investor? What are the monies being spent on?

C. Capital equipment list

1. What major and minor equipment will you use in the business?

D. Pro forma cash flow statement

1. Is your business seasonal?

2. Do your purchases, advertising expenses, personnel costs, and other variable costs reflect this seasonality?

3. Can the business sustain itself over the slow sales periods?

4. Can you afford to repay the debt of a loan and still survive? (Most financial institutions will require a 3-year cash flow projection, while some will ask for best, most likely, and worst case scenarios.

E. Assumptions

1. Explains/justifies the cash flow projection figures

F. Pro forma profit and loss statement

1. Summarizes projected gross sales, cost of services, expenses

G. Pro forma balance sheet

    1. Summarizes projected assets, liabilities, and net worth

H. Personal financial statement

    1. Have you made wise personal financial decisions?

    2. Do you have resources to call upon if business cash flow is poor?

    3. How will the loan be collateralized?

I. Personal income tax returns (last three years)

    1. Required for financial proposals

VIII. Supporting Documents

This area includes documentation to uphold what you have concluded in other areas of your plan. Sample letters of recommendation, market research, equipment bids, sales agreements, etc. along with other information that will be specific to your business plan are examples.

IX. Personalized Cover Letter

All business plans should have an executive summary or sometimes called a cover letter attached, addressed to the party or parties from which funding is being requested. It should clearly state the amount of money required and the purpose for which it will be used. The letter will need to also briefly mention collateral and any investment you will be providing. Once you have your business plan together and your cover letter written, you have taken the first important step toward obtaining funding for your organization!

5

Don't wait for your ship to come in, swim out to it.

--- **Anon**

Sources of Money to Start Your Business

Start-up Funding Sources

Once you have computed your initial capital requirements, where will you get the money? Your first source is your personal savings, then relatives, friends or other individuals who may be interested in your venture. Before bringing others into your venture from outside sources, remember you should have personal control of enough of your business to assure ownership. Assuming that you do not have enough capital to meet all of the start-up requirements of your new business, let us take a look at the major sources of start-up capital and how you go about creating investment interest.

Simple Loans

So, what are your capital choices? Let's start with simple loans. Your first source of capital will probably be a loan from yourself. Most businesses are founded with cash from the founder's pocketbook. Sure, there are simple advantages here: pure control and ownership. You own the whole company, control the show, and stand to reap the gains should your venture become valuable. Great.

But there's a huge potential downside here as well. Even the best-researched and well-run startups involve risk. And you are putting your assets on the line. It's great to read about risk-takers who take out second mortgages on their homes and borrow from their retirement funds to launch businesses that turn them into millionaires. There are far fewer stories in the news about the many people who take great risks -- and fail. And unfortunately, these stories are very real and very common. So while I believe you need to trust yourself, and take the leap, be sure to consider (and reconsider!) the risk of your venture carefully when investing your own money.

There are wild stories of individuals who turn to credit cards for their startup capital. Sure, in our credit-easy economy, credit cards represent an easy form of quick cash, one that many starting entrepreneurs exploit -- especially when they come with low rates. Yet the eventual high rates and lack of any other support rate them low on the list of sources.

Small Business Administration

This agency was created to help businesses in many ways, of which lending money is their largest and most important function. It is rare that the SBA will actually lend money themselves, instead, they will partner with a bank by guaranteeing part of the loan in a range of 50% to 90% depending on the situation. The SBA has several loan programs, and your bank will determine which one is the best for you. It is a good deal for the bank because the SBA is taking much of the risk out of the loan by its guarantee. You will find that some banks aggressively pursue SBA loans and others do not want to bother with them. Usually the older, more conservative banks do not want them, whereas the younger, more aggressive banks will welcome them. Your first step is to call the SBA office in your area and ask them who their "Preferred Lenders" are. Then call one of those banks and ask to speak to the loan officer who handles SBA loans. If they don't have one, hang up and keep calling until you find one that does. Schedule an appointment. Before you go in to see them however, ask the SBA office to send you the SBA loan package, or better yet, go in and pick it up from them. This will give you an outline of what you will need for the bank loan officer and the information that they will look for in your "Business Plan." The follow are some of the more popular SBA loan programs

7(a) Loan Guaranty Program

The 7(a) Loan Guaranty Program is the SBA's primary loan program. The eligibility requirements and credit criteria of the program are very broad in order to accommodate a wide range of financing needs. When a small business applies to a lending institution for a loan, the lender reviews the application and decides if it merits a loan on its own or if it requires additional support in the form of an SBA guaranty. The lender then requests SBA backing on the loan. In guaranteeing the loan, the SBA assures the lender that, in the event the borrower does not repay the loan, the government will reimburse the lending institution for a portion of its loss. By providing this guaranty, the SBA is able to help tens of thousands of small businesses every year get financing they would not otherwise obtain.

To qualify for an SBA guaranty, a small business must meet the 7(a) criteria, and the lender must certify that it could not provide funding on reasonable terms except with an SBA guaranty. The SBA can guarantee as much as 85 percent on loans of up to $150,000 and 75 percent on loans of more than $150,000. In most cases, the maximum guaranty is $1 million. Exceptions are the International Trade, DELTA and 504 loan programs, which have higher loan limits. The maximum total loan size under the 7(a) program is $2 million.

LowDoc

LowDoc is one of SBA's most popular programs. Once you have met your lender's requirements for credit, LowDoc offers a simple, one-page SBA application form and rapid turnaround on approvals for loans up to $150,000 (for loans over $50,000, you must also provide a copy of U.S. Income Tax Schedule C or the front page of the corporate or partnership returns for the past three years). The SBA will guarantee up to 85 percent of the loan amount. The SBA processes applications quickly, usually within two or three business days. Proceeds may not be used to repay certain types of existing debt. Business start-ups, as well as businesses with average annual sales for the past three years not exceeding $5 million and with 100 or fewer employees, including affiliates, are eligible.

SBA 504 Loan Program

504 is the SBA's economic development instrument that supports American small business growth and helps

communities through business expansion and job creation. The SBA 504 loan program provides long-term, fixed rate, subordinate mortgage financing for acquisition and/or renovation of capital assets including land, buildings and equipment. Virtually all types of for-profit small businesses are eligible for this program.

The SBA 504 loan is distinguished from other SBA loan programs in these ways:

- Lower down payment; allows a business to conserve valuable operating capital by injecting just 10% of total project cost.

- Fixed interest rate; borrower knows cost of occupancy for the next 20 years.

- Rate is usually below market rate.

- All project costs can be financed, including acquisition (land and building, land and construction of building, renovations, machinery and equipment) and soft costs such as title insurance, legal, appraisal, environmental and bridge loan fees. Closing costs may be financed.

- Collateral is typically assets financed; allows other assets to be free of liens and available to secure other needed financing.

- Long-term: real estate loans are 20-year term, heavy equipment 10 or 20-year terms and are self-amortizing.

- The 504 Program encourages banks and other lenders to make loans in first position on practical terms, help them retain growing clients, and provides CRA credit.

- 504 Program benefits the borrower's community through job creation and retention. Businesses that receive 504 loans are small net worth under

$6 million, net profit after taxes under $2 million, or meet other SBA size standards.

- Organized as for profit.

- Any type of business retail, service, wholesale or manufacturing.

The SBA's 504 lending intermediaries, Certified Development Companies (CDCs) serve your community to finance business expansion needs through 504. Their professional staffs work directly with you to tailor a financing package that meets program guidelines and the credit capacity of your business. The 504 Loan Program is the first national financing program specifically designed for expanding small business whose investment will create jobs.

Small Business Development Center (SBDC)

Call your local SBDC and find out if there are any Small Business Investment Corporations (SBIC), or Minority Enterprise Business Investment Corporations (MESBIC) in your area. Also ask them about the availability of State or Regional funding groups who you could talk to about your start-up needs. They can also give you information about several National Women's Associations who can lead you to lending resources. The SBDC can also help you in the preparation of your business plan and provide follow-on guidance for your business.

Your Local Bank

Banks are not as flexible in granting loans to start-up businesses as they once were. This is not the fault of your bank but of the Federal Government Laws that greatly restrict what your bank can and cannot do in lending money. The bank needs to fully secure a business start-up loan and that is generally done with 100% of your personal assets, home, cars, property, savings, etc. Your assets will mitigate the bank's losses if your business fails. This is why an SBA loan is worth considering because while the bank will still require a lot of collateral, they know they have the SBA guarantee to fall back on.

It is important to have the bank on your side because you will need a business checking account with them. If you can, deal with a bank you are already doing business with. You may need for them to give you a line of credit someday and it is possible that you may need them to loan you money on your accounts receivable and there may be other credits you will require. Get to know your banker on a first name basis. Openly discuss your plans and difficulties. Keep him or her informed about every aspect of your business and provides them with financial statements every six months even if they do not require them. Get to know the management policies of your bank. Know if your maximum requirements fall within the bank's legal limits. If you need financial help carefully prepare, in printed form, complete information that will present a thorough understanding of your entire proposition. Many business people destroy their chances of getting financial help by failing to present their proposition properly. Ask your banker what they look for in a proposal and follow their guidelines very carefully.

Trade Supplier or Equipment Manufacturer.

Companies from which you buy equipment, uniforms, office supplies etc, may also furnish capital to you in terms of extended credit. Equipment vendors all have lease programs that will enable you to leverage the equipment as an asset while you "rent" the equipment for an agreed period of time, and at the end of that period you buy the equipment. This can range from one dollar to the fair market value of the equipment at the end of the lease. Many lease programs will allow you to "bundle" all of your requirements into one master lease, so you can include build-out, furniture, office equipment, etc. in addition to other needs. This is an excellent way to get your Non-Medical Home Care business started because it allows you to pay for the things you need out of future income.

6

To hell with circumstances, I create opportunities.
--- **Bruce Lee**

Marketing: How to Create Interest in Your Services

Marketing Your Non-Medical Home Care Service

For Non-Medical Home Care clients, the motivations are all about taking care of someone that they care about. What drives those motivations is comfort level with you. Your potential client wants to FEEL like you care.
It is easy to write about the services that you offer. It is much harder to dig down deep and use your words to turn marketing collateral material into a meaningful message that your company is

the company that they want to trust to take care of someone that they love.

Don't' just explain your services, talk about them and why you offer them. Before any client does business with you as a Non-Medical Home Care professional, they want to know that this is more than just a profession for you, and that they will be more than just a replaceable business opportunity. By contracting with you, they are offering to let you into their home to take care of them or someone that they care about.

As with any message, you can go overboard with the message of care. Trying to make the case that the parent is as well off with you as they are with their family probably isn't going to win you any new friends... or clients! Family caregivers want to be supported, not replaced.

This is not to say however, that you can abandon professionalism in working with your clients. You can be the most wonderfully personal and nice person that they have talked to, but if they sense that you lack professional courtesy and responsibility, it is all for nothing. If they wanted to just hire a really nice person, there is probably an unemployed cousin somewhere in the family who would gladly sit around and collect a paycheck. Professionalism is an absolute must.

Better Business Tip

Avoid gimmicky and clever advertising. Center your message on the benefits and advantages of your Non-Medical Home Care service -- such as experience and reliability – rather than making emotional appeals.

Establishing Your Advertising Budget

Deciding how much your advertising should cost - including how much should be invested in making sales grow - and how that amount should be allocated is completely up to you.

Advertising costs are a completely controllable expense. Advertising budgets are the means of determining and controlling this expense and dividing it wisely among departments, lines or services.

This business guide describes various methods (percentage of sales or profits, units of sales, objective and task) of establishing an advertising budget and suggests ways of applying budget amounts to get the effect you want.

If you want to build sales, it is almost certain that you will need to advertise. How much should you spend? How should you allocate your advertising dollars? How can you be sure your advertising outlays aren't out of line? The advertising budget helps you determine how much you have to spend as well as how you are going to spend it.

What you would like to invest in advertising and what you can afford are seldom the same. Spending too much is obviously an extravagance, but spending too little can be just as bad in terms of lost sales and diminished visibility. Costs must be tied to results. You must be prepared to evaluate your goals and assess your capabilities - a budget will help you do precisely this.

Your budget will help you choose and assess the amount of advertising and its timing. It will also serve as the background for next year's plan.

Methods of Establishing a Budget.

Each of The various ways in which to establish an advertising budget has its problems as well as its benefits. No method is perfect for all types of businesses, nor for that matter is any combination of methods.

Below, concepts from several traditional methods of budgeting have been combined into three basic methods: percentage of sales or profits, unit of sales, and objective and task. You will need to use judgement and caution in choosing your method or methods.

Percentage of Sales or Profits

The most widely used method of establishing an advertising budget is to base it on a percentage of sales. Advertising is as much a business expense as, say, the cost of labor and, thus, should be related to the quantity of sales dollars.

The percentage-of-sales method avoids some of the problems that result from using profits as a base. For instance, if profits in a period are low, it might not be the fault of sale or advertising. But if you stick with the same percentage figure, you will automatically reduce your advertising allotment. There's no way around it: two percent of $10 000 is less than two percent of $15 000.

Such a cut in the advertising budget, if profits are down for other reasons, may very well lead to further losses in sales and profits. This in turn will lead to further reductions in advertising investment, and so on.

In the short run a small business owner might make small additions to profit by cutting advertising expenses, but such a policy could lead to a long-term deterioration of the bottom line. By using the percentage-of-sales method, you keep your advertising in a consistent relation to your sales volume - which is what your advertising should be primarily affecting. Gross margin, especially over the long run, should also show an increase, of course, if your advertising outlays are being properly applied.

<u>What percentage?</u>
You can guide your choice of a percentage-of-sales figure by finding out what other businesses in your industry are doing. These percentages are fairly consistent within the Non-Medical Home Care sector.

It is fairly easy to figure out the ratio of advertising expense to sales in your industry. You can find these ratios through:

- Web sites such as Bizminer
  http://www.bizminer.com

- Reports published by financial institutions such as Dun & Bradstreet at: http://www.dnb.com.

- Knowing the advertising sales ratio for your industry will help you spend proportionately to your competitors. You must be careful however, not to base your entire budget on these reads. Every situation is slightly different and industry averages are not gospel. Your particular situation may require you to advertise more or less than your competition. You may feel that at this point in your business life cycle, it is important to spend more than average on advertising. The decision is ultimately yours. After all, growth requires investment.

  No business owner should let any method bind him or her. It may be helpful for you to use the percentage-of-sales method because it is quick and easy. Not only is it a sound method for stable markets, but it may also keep your advertising budget from getting way out of proportion. Note: if you are looking to expand your market share, you will probably have to use a larger percentage of sales toward advertising than the industry average.

What sales? Your budget can be determined as a percentage of past sales, of estimated future sales, or as a combination of the two.

Your base can be last year's sales or an average of a number of years in the immediate past. Consider, though, that changes in economic conditions may cause your figures to be too high or too low.

You can calculate your advertising budget as a percentage of your anticipated sales for next year. The most common pitfall of this method is an optimistic assumption that your business will continue to grow. You must always keep general business trends in mind, especially if there is the chance of a slump. Remember to assess the directions in both the industry and your own operation.

The middle ground between a conservative appraisal based on last year's sales and an often overly optimistic assessment of next year's, is to combine both. This method is generally more realistic during periods of changing economic conditions. It allows you to analyze trends and results as well as predict future sales with a little more accurately.

Objective and Task
The most difficult (and least used) method for determining an advertising budget is the objective-and-task approach. Though it is more

complex (and therefore less attractive) than other methods, this approach is the most accurate and therefore best method for determining your budget.

It relates the appropriation to the marketing task to be accomplished.

It relates the advertising appropriation under usual conditions and in the long run to the volume of sales, so that profits and reserves will not be drained.

To establish your budget using this method, you need a coordinated marketing program with specific objectives based on a thorough survey of your markets and their potential.

- While the percentage-of-sales or profits method first determines how much you'll spend without much consideration of what you want to accomplish, the task method establishes what you must do in order to meet your objectives. Only then do you calculate its cost.

  You should set specific objectives: not just "Increase sales", but, for example, "Sell 25 percent more of service Y by attracting the business of clients in area X". Then determine what media best reaches your target market and estimate how much it will cost to run the number and types of advertisements you think it'll take to get that sales increase. You repeat this process for each of your objectives. When you total these costs, you have your projected budget.

  Of course, you may find that you can't afford to advertise, as you'd like to. It's a good idea, therefore, to rank your objectives. As with the

other methods, be prepared to change your plan
to reflect reality and to fit the resources you have
available.

Calendar Periods

Most executives of small businesses usually plan
their advertising on a monthly or weekly basis.
Your budget, even if it is for a longer planning
period, should also be calculated for these shorter
periods. It will give you better control.

The percentage-of-sales method is also useful
here to determine how much money to allocate by
time periods. The standard practice is to match
sales with advertising dollars. Thus, if February
accounts for 5 percent of your sales, you might
give it 5 percent of your budget.

Sometimes you might want to adjust advertising
allocations downward in some of your heavier
sales months, so you can boost the budget of
some of your poorer periods. But this should be
done only if you have reason (as when you
competition's sales trends differ markedly from
yours) to believe that a change in your advertising
timing could improve slow sales.

Media

The amount of advertising that you place in each
advertising medium - direct mail, newspapers,
radio, etc. - should be determined by past
experience, industry practice, and ideas from
media specialists. Normally it is wise to use the
same sort of media your competitors use. That is
most likely where your potential clients look and
listen.

Sales Areas

You can either spend your advertising dollars in
areas where your clients already frequent, or you

can use them to stimulate new sales areas. Whatever you choose, remember that it is usually more costly to develop new markets than it is to maintain the ones that are already established.

A Flexible Budget
Any combination of these methods may be employed in the formation and allocation of your advertising budget. Based on your advertising needs, you may find that you need all or only one of these methods to meet your advertising objectives. Whatever the case, make sure that your budget is flexible. It must be easy to adjust when there are changes in the market.

The duration of your planning and budgeting period depends upon your business. If you can use short budgeting periods, you'll find that your advertising can be more flexible and that you can change tactics to meet immediate trends.

To ensure advertising flexibility, you should have a contingency fund to deal with special circumstances - such as the introduction of a new service, specials available in local media, or unexpected competitive situations.

Beware of your competitors' activities at all times. Don't blindly copy your competitors, but analyze how their actions may affect your business - and be prepared to act.

Your first budget will be the most difficult to develop - but it will be worth the effort since it will help you analyze the results of your advertising. By your next business year you will have a more factual basis for budgeting than you did before. Your plans will become more effective with each budget you develop.

Selling Your Non-Medical Home Care Expertise

You've advertised and promoted your business. You've mapped out your business plan, and worked hard to project a professional image. What next? When the potential client walks into your office or calls on the telephone, you must now convince that individual into accepting the Non-Medical Home Care services you have to offer. Selling your expertise is even more imperative especially if YOU took the initiative to contact a prospective client first. So don't sit back but take the necessary steps to secure that job.

Once you have an interested party, there are certain guidelines you must follow to be effective and to be able to close that sale, too. We will examine the initial impression, determination of the client's needs, the sales presentation, and the closing of that sale. Word-of-mouth advertising and good public relations are often the best ways of promoting a Non-Medical Home Care service. Networking, including an open-house day for those in the health field of your region such as employees from hospitals, clinics, pharmacies and community services, can be a useful way to promote your establishment. These employees should be able to answer questions from seniors looking for Non-Medical Home Care services. Also, bear in mind that a happy client or family is also a very good method of advertising.

The Print and Graphic Arts Media
Brochures and posters are cost effective ways to provide a combination of moving and static visual impact with the most versatile applications. Brochures inform and posters inspire the client.

Business pages of the telephone book provide an

interactive link to the primary electronic media, the telephone and the fax. The toll free 1-800 service invites extended markets, and implies modern services.

Business cards and stationery are effective, inexpensive and professional promotional tools but use of these items should be restricted to personal contacts. Rubber stamps or staples are for impersonal, routine tasks and should not be used in any way with this media. Advertising specialties such as pens, key rings and calendars acknowledge goodwill in the form of a small gift, but these convey more image than information.

Many Non-Medical Home Care providers prefer local newspapers because it provides maximum flexibility in terms of budget, timing, coupon feedback and price mix. The perception rate is high because the reader can get more than one impact from the same message. Although printed advertising can be the most costly avenue, this form of exposure puts your name and message in front of the largest number of likely clients. Selecting and designing your advertisement should be given the priority it deserves. Look at other printed advertising to evaluate why it commanded your attention. Is there something you can use in your advertisement? Pay attention to copy, graphics, type style, and use of space. Note the ad's placement on the page and the section it's found in. Why do certain types of businesses run their ads in specific sections of the newspaper? Results! You can use what drew your interest and modify it to suit your business' needs. Being innovative and the first to try something new is best left up to media professionals. Blunders can blow your budget. To be effective with your advertising dollars, you must target the appropriate audience. Who exactly do you want to reach? Different audiences are targeted through different publications. So which publication you advertise in is a fundamental decision. Remember, the local newspaper usually covers ALL households in an area and you pay for this mass-marketing privilege. Is there another local newsletter, publication, or magazine better suited to the market you're covering? In addition, will some of these publications offer a special rate for consecutive advertising or for running an ad in a particular business page section that is published periodically?

After you've targeted the market, think of why potential clients need your service. What benefit will they receive? Make sure you point this out in your ad using a headline, or a graphic. Why should they call or act now? Put a time limit on your special offer. Extend an additional bonus service, or highlight a special price if they call within a certain period. If you are running a "special", advertise as many times as profitable to be consistent and get the most exposure. People respond to a repeated message, not to scattered, occasional advertising. Market research notes that for every three advertisements scanned, the average consumer ignores two. That means you need to run a specific ad directed toward a specific niche several times before it is noticed, and therefore your company, is remembered. The Non-Medical Home Care industry requires that you continuously target your prospects with radio spots, newspaper ads, or direct mailings.

Effective penetration requires sticking with an ad or campaign long after you've grown sick of viewing it. In the big parade of marketing, don't get off the float just because you're tired of all that time spent designing, constructing, and riding it along the route. Remember, every face in the crowd deserves a chance to see your endeavor.

Never drop an ad or campaign that's still pulling in those calls. For example, if after every direct mail initiative your sales rocket, why derail a sure marketing method? When your clients mention they heard your advertisement on a radio spot, why try to reinvent the wheel? Your advertising is working. Now just do it ... again!

Well, do you ever try a new approach? Of course you should test a distinctive, but different, advertising campaign while still running the old one. In the meantime, consider cutting down on your tried-and-true ad's size or repositioning it to save on cost. Then evaluate and compare client response between the old and new initiative. Don't jump ship until the evidence is clear to do so!

Yes, repetition is the mother of response when it comes to your marketing campaign. So, could you just repeat that ... please?

The Electronic Media
Radio is cost effective and the audiences are routinely loyal to a station's program format. The lack of visual impact makes the message more personal and conversational. Promotional events often build on the interactive links with the audience. Radio messages tend to develop a personality and convey a friendly, local relationship.

Television captures more audience time than any other medium and it has the powerful advantages of visual impact. It is generally believed that as much as 90% of a person's total perception is the result of images conveyed to the brain in one way or another.

The TV commercial is targeted at a home audience in a relaxed and suggestive atmosphere, by using short, repetitive, and high impact messages. The TV remote control has changed viewing habits such that commercial spots are now formatted in clusters of ten and fifteen second clips.

There are an increasing number of online directories available with which you can list your business. Not only are many of these directories available at reasonable rates, they allow clients from all parts of your region and state easy access to your business.

The Personal Efforts

Networking and Word of Mouth referrals are an effective way to reduce out of pocket costs and cultivate a clientele. The valued opinion of influential clients is the most important and cost effective promotion that your business can develop. Markets will never buy your services; only clients buy services.

Community involvement expands the personal network of contacts and marketing intelligence; however, this should be the by-product of genuine interest in the community.

Special promotions and events can be made to work in concert with any one or a combination of the above methods. This can be in the form of prizes, Welcome Wagon gifts, free passes, free coffee etc.

Better Business Tip

Network. It's easy to become isolated in a small business. Force yourself to go out and meet people who can provide business support. Contact with others will motivate you and help generate new ideas.

Your Telephone: A Powerful Sales Tool

The business telephone is an incredible sales and image-making tool that's already at your fingertips. Take time to consider a professional backdrop by assessing where, when and how your telephone will be used and answered.

Where will you place your business telephone? If you are in a home office setting, consider whether you will use your own personal line or install a separate business line. The advantage of the latter is that you will know which calls are personal and which ones are for business purposes. Then you'll be able to answer confidently, "Jo Anne's Home Care", instead of just, "Hello".

If you are already in an office, be sure to place your telephone away from unnecessary noise. This way, each client's call can be given the dignity and priority it deserves.

How should you answer the telephone? Answer each call clearly by identifying the name of your business and by supplying YOUR name as well. Write down each client's name, telephone number and nature of the call. By writing their name down, not only will you have a record of it later, but also you can project a confident image through the use of their name in the ensuing conversation. Using the client's name in your conversation projects a professional yet warm impression.

When should you answer the telephone? You MUST answer or provide a means by which a client can contact you during the hours you are open. On the occasions that you will be away from the office, use an answering machine or service. An alternative would be to redirect your calls to a mobile phone. Always return calls left on your answering machine the same day, if not as soon as possible. A client wishing to use your service can easily change their mind and call another company if you delay.

Words communicate, convince, and ultimately sell, but timing is everything. So don't jump in and start preaching the moment they take a breath. If there's anything a client can't stand it's sitting through a sermon about what they really need when they feel they really don't need it. Even if they really do! You're probably not going to convince them immediately anyway. Stay away from saying, "I think you need to" "This is really what you should do."

Instead, listen to the client, not yourself. Try using reassurances such as, "Our job is to help you." "We'll make every effort to assist you." "We're committed to providing the level of service you deserve." What if those phrases just don't seem right for you? Then use simple clauses such as, "Yes, I see what you mean." "I understand."

When it's finally your turn to talk, start painting vivid pictures in the client's mind. Describe the quality of your services. Speak of how your services can specific solve the client's problems. Show the client what's in it for him or her. You get the idea. The more you practice, the easier it'll become. Just try to be balanced and not get carried away with your new vocabulary, though. Too much flowery speech may make them tune you out, or worse yet, make them suspicious that you're trying to pull a fast one.

Below is a telephone strategy you can use to ensure you and your employee projects the best image. Take it upon yourself to...

1. Present a pleasant demeanor. Don't allow anyone at your business to answer the telephone gruffly with a 'Yeah?' Instead, have all identify your business clearly as well as themselves.

2. Make sure no one eats or chews gum while on the telephone. And, make sure no one flips through papers or reading e-mails, either. Doing so portrays disinterest and disrespect.

3. Try to return calls within the first 24 hours. That builds client confidence.

4. Ask the client whether it's a good time to talk when placing or returning a call. Be as brief as possible. If the conversation exceeds 10 minutes or so, another appointment could be made.

5. Take a minute to organize thoughts before making an important call. If needed, practice what's going to be said out loud.

6. Be conversational. Less talking and more listening, give time to respond at appropriate intervals. Let the client know that what they're saying is important.

In addition, take action to ensure that your Non-Medical Home Care business is portrayed at its best. The voice that answers your company's telephone has a responsibility to depict a certain personality. Well, is it likable? Friendly? Confident? It should be!
How can you get an idea of the image your company? Have a trusted associate telephone your office and make an honest evaluation. What immediate impression do they get? Have them assess...

1. Whether the person answering the telephone can be heard comfortably. Is the voice too soft? Too loud? Volume is the first but most important factor.

2. If the voice on the other end is strained. When
    someone lacks confidence, nervousness can make
    listening to the delivery uncomfortable.

3. Whether the person speaks in a monotone. Pitch
    is the spice of speech. It keeps clients interested
    in what's being said.

4. If the voice is too rapid or too slow. Speaking too
    quickly may not enable your listeners to
    understand the message. Speaking too slowly is
    another great way to put them to sleep.

5. Whether the person has good articulation. Are
    their words pronounced correctly and clearly?
    Unfortunately, sloppy speech can present your
    business as one that's unknowledgeable and
    careless.

Remember to use your telephone as the powerful sales
tool that it already is. Develop strategies and take
action. Your clients will reward you!

Using Low-Cost, High-Impact Selling Tools

Stationery and Business card

Your stationery and business card can do a respectable
job in representing you when you aren't available in
person. These may be professionally printed for the best
appearance with your company name, logo, address,
telephone number, email address and web site.

Operating on a budget? There are many options
available such as rubber stamps. These can be used to
individually mark or stamp each envelope, letterhead or
card. This is not recommended because it may portray
an image of being a small fish in a big pond. If you

choose to use them, just make sure you do it neatly! Or, try some of the latest custom-looking stationery available at office supply stores. These can work with many computer printers. So, try your hand at customizing your own look right from your own computer. Business Invoices used by you can also be handled this way. Local or mail order companies offer many options to personalize these within a price range you can afford.

Classified Ads

Not to be forgotten is the low-cost classified ad section of the local newspaper. This can be extremely productive because your presence will be encountered daily. Check into running an ad in the business services section right within the classifieds, or place a few lines under one of the other headings.

Press Release

Did you know you could receive some free advertising? Yes. A great one-time, free advertising promotion is called a press release. It won't cost you a penny, either. This is run in the newspaper and serves as an announcement. For example, a press release can be run upon your grand opening. Briefly describe your company and what services it offers. Be certain to include your company's name, address, and phone number. A photo of you at your business location would complement the copy. Don't forget to mention your opening date, too. Additionally, press releases can be issued whenever you offer a new service, attend an industry seminar, or promote employees within your organization. Highlight how the community will benefit from the continuing education or new service.

<u>How to Write a Release</u>

Although a press release is 'straight news', it is still important to be creative in the way that information is presented. Ponder over what would make a release unique or relevant to your audience. Develop a theme and keep it simple. Focus on only one point, initiative, or individual.

When writing a release, get to the main points quickly. News demands a 'lead'. The lead is usually within the first sentence. A professional journalist typically answers who, what, where, why, when and how immediately. There will be plenty of time to bolster the fundamentals by adding embellishments later.

Make sure your writing is uncomplicated and active. An un-expressive read will simply not be remembered. Take care about using technical or industry-specific terminology unless you are submitting the information to a trade journal.

Include quotations in a press release for added interest. They add flavor or and present the facts from a different vantage point. Besides being accurate, quotes should flow with the development of the story. And, please, resist the urge to use them as a sales tool. Remember two helpful hints about quotations: 1. Don't begin a release with a quote. 2. Make sure quotations make their own paragraph. Just add the attribution either before the quote or after.

A press release with even the most engaging content needs to follow a few format formulas. These guidelines are simple, yet necessary.

Print a release on company letterhead. Include a contact name and telephone number.

State when a release is scheduled for publication. Although most press releases are printed immediately, you can request a hold on the information or have it 'embargoed' until a certain date. This is appropriate if you are reporting on a seminar or an opening that is set for a certain date.

Place a headline or title at the top of the body of a press release. The title should summarize the information contained. The media may use it or they may modify it, but supplying one will convey the main theme you wish to emphasize.

Format the body of a press release with margins of approximately one inch. Double-space it and type 'more' at the bottom of your first page in case you need to add another. Try to keep the length of an entire release down to two pages. Remember a press release is not an article.

Finally, ask someone who's proficient in spelling and grammar to proofread your release. Don't have a press release turned away because it doesn't project a professional image.

<u>The Telephone Directory</u>

The local telephone directory is a publication that will be one of your earliest and primary advertising mediums. Most businesses that advertise in the yellow pages find it profitable to do so. Since your potential clients all have a telephone book on hand, allocate a portion of your advertising expense to include this avenue of promotion.

Many telephone directory salespeople can offer suggestions for an eye-catching display ad. Their suggestions, along with a sampling of other yellow page ads, will give you a wealth of ideas.

<u>Word of Mouth</u>

Reputation can precede you! Satisfied and happy clients can do more to promote your business than the most expensive, flashiest ads. In this sense, talk really is cheap.

Just ONE client can tell several acquaintances about you and steer their dollars your way. Take advantage of this avenue by leaving additional business cards that the client can pass along.

Remember, a good name comes only by being fair in price, delivering quality service, and adjusting any problems promptly. These three things will create a solid business relationship and a profitable one, too.

<u>Building and Vehicle Identification</u>
Have you considered the impact that your signs have on your business?

This business guide discusses signs, what they can do for your business, and how they can be used to your advantage. A checklist for ordering a business sign is also provided. Signs are one of the most efficient and effective means of communication. Signs help people find you, they reach people who are passing by your establishment or vehicle, and they present an image of your business. In short, signs tell people who you are and what you are selling.

Your building and vehicle signs are an advertisement themselves. Clean, professional building and vehicle identification signs must be given the priority they deserve to assure your potential client that your really know your "P's & Q's".

Always be sure to check with local zoning ordinances as to limitations. Recently many communities have enacted specific guidelines as to what size, quantity, and location this identification can assume. Additionally, if your office is located in a residential area, you may not be able to erect or display a sign outside your home.

Vehicle identification can be permanent or portable. Vinyl lettering can be applied either directly to the vehicle or on magnetic material that can be removed at will. Simple, direct signage that conveys your specific type of work is best since your sign is going to be on the move. Your name and/or logo should also take priority, as this is what most people will remember first. A telephone number or address is secondary. If your vehicle sign attracts and makes an impression, be assured they'll look your name up in the telephone book when the need arises.

Signs are such a powerful communication medium that it is difficult to estimate the extent of their influence. Other media require the directed attention of the person receiving the message. Signs, however, can convey a message while creating a mood or feeling of atmosphere. It is not necessary for people to give full attention to your sign in order to derive meaning from its presence. A sign is the most direct form of visual communication available. In fact, so many people use signs without a second thought that it is easy to overlook their importance. When we cannot talk to other people directly in a given location, we tack up signs: wet paint, beware of dog, enter here, garage sale, etc. Signs are the only form of mass communication directly available to everyone.

<u>Networking.</u>
No, we're not referring to the process of linking several computer workstations together. Instead, we're talking about the ability to meet clients and establish relationships with them. Why? Because networking, commonly called "working the room", is really an astute means by which either a start-up or a veteran Non-Medical Home Care service provider can promote or expand their business.

How clever is it? Well, it virtually costs you nothing but it can certainly bring in the work. Now that's an intelligent way to develop a customer base!

Don't get the idea that that means you have to act like an artificially happy salesperson hawking your wares at every opportunity. Nothing could be farther from the truth. A good networker is someone who honestly believes in his or her abilities and in the benefits their service can provide. And that conviction shows beyond anything that they can possibly assert as well.

In order to network effectively you need to take advantage of opportunities to meet new people. Where are these opportunities? Well, normal business functions can become an arena to sensibly interact with potential clients. Look to luncheons, conventions, local organizational meetings, and community events as avenues that can yield ongoing relationships even lucrative ones.

But there's more. To "work the room" and receive results, you have to take a positive proactive approach. That means that you can't sit back and expect a payoff just because you're present. Here are some suggestions to try:

Set objectives. Whether your goal is to meet at least 3 new people or to learn something new that you can carry back to enhance your business, make sure the time is well spent. If you want to make new acquaintances, don't sit with the same old crowd. And if you want to learn and benefit from innovative ideas, don't be afraid to ask questions.

Stay on your feet as much as you can. If you sit down too early, you'll miss meeting others. Time to mingle is precious because that meeting or dinner will start all too soon! Remember what you're there for.

Do something to help others. At the event, could you ask the host or hostess if they need assistance? Or, could you take it upon yourself to help a few businesspeople to get to know others? Introduce them to those you've already met. After all, they're there for the same reasons you are and they'll be eternally grateful to you!

Take your business cards. When that important conversation turns to you, have something on hand that others can remember you by. Just remember to be discreet.

Well then, are you ready to "work the room" and reap the results? If you're ready to network, you can take advantage of a clever way to develop, promote or expand your business. Investigate all the avenues at your disposal that can yield lucrative rewards and plan to utilize them effectively. Forge ongoing relationships by setting objectives, mingling with others, and assisting them when you can. And of course, be alert to leave your business card when it's appropriate!

Speaking Opportunities

A means to enlarge your market is already at the tip of your tongue! What is it? Why it's the speaking opportunity, an effective public relations tool!

Whether addressing a few at a roundtable discussion or many at a keynote function, a speaking engagement can reach potential clients. As you go about your daily routine, think of the businesses you pass ... the attorney's office, a medical complex, nursing homes etc. How can you approach these markets in a dignified manner? Yes, you could 'cold call' to sell your services but a more acceptable way could be by taking advantage of a speaking opportunity. Show these how your services benefit the community and in a roundabout way, how your services can reach and educate their own clientele.

Many associations and trade organizations host seminars, conferences and shows. Of these, some are actively searching for guest speakers that can address their particular audience. Schools, colleges, and universities invite businesspersons and executives to speak to their students, teachers, and organizations.

Identify your audience and select material that would benefit and interest them. Ask the conference organizer for some background of the market you're going to address. Make sure your approach contains quality, not necessarily quantity information. Above all, shun the urge to include a sales pitch.

Delivering A Perfect Sales Presentation

A sales presentation cannot begin without an assessment of the client's Home Care needs. First, LOOK, LISTEN, and LEARN. Then suggests solutions. Listening to what the clients have in mind conveys an interest in his particular needs. YOU may be the Non-Medical Home Care expert, but your CLIENT knows what best for them or their love ones. Also, listen to what your client can afford. Keep a few guidelines in mind when preparing your presentation.

If you haven't already gathered background information about your client do so immediately. To be effective, you have to know what appeals to the client you're going to address. Your presentation should be an open discussion, so try to anticipate questions and prepare responses. Be ready so you won't be thrown by a tough question.

After gathering the preceding information, you should be able to present a satisfactory service solution that addresses the client's concerns. Offer each particular solutions one step at a time. By doing this, each response can be met individually to determine what is best for him and which solution he likes the best. Your sales presentation should be relaxed and unhurried. Take the time to answer any questions along the way. Additionally, dress appropriately. Put yourself, as well as your client at ease by wearing the right clothes. This is a key non-verbal aspect of delivering a successful presentation.

When you feel confident that all the questions have been answered and the client has been sold on the quality of your services, finalizing their decision is the next step. Closing the sale can be very simple if it is done by asking a question such as, "When did you say you would like us to start providing assistance?" or "Let's write your request so that we can get you some assistance". Then, pull out your client contract. This will smoothly guide the client onto that next step. Accurately spelling out your payment terms is vital so that no future misunderstandings ensue.

Whether you "sold" the client or not, you should evaluate your performance. If you received the contract, note what you feel was the determining factor in convincing that client to buy your service. Was your sales presentation organized and thorough? Did you offer a variety of solutions and let him make the decision?

If you did not receive the sale, ask yourself why you think the client did not respond. As in a cold call, did you call at the wrong time? Was it not within his budget? Did you listen to his needs and respond to them?

Always keep a positive attitude, as this will reflect on your confidence with the next sales presentation. No one can sell services EVERY time! Your outlook will be a factor in wanting to improve and polish your sales technique.

The Follow Up Call -- A Simple Step to Increased Sales

By ignoring a critical, yet simple step, the goal of increased sales could be slipping through your very fingers. On the other hand, by using a technique that requires just a small investment of time you can yield impressive bottom-line results. That approach is the follow up.

Just think ... when was the last time you contacted a previous client or touched base again with a prospective client? Do you find yourself assuming that the client must take your relationship to the next stage? Even after an initial presentation that went well or a job that was completed satisfactorily, keeping your presence in front of the client is up to you. After all, when communication between you and the client is concluded, he will likely go back to his normal routine. In addition, they may choose the Non-Medical Home Care business that follow up and ask for their business.

First, focus on your previous clients, the ones with whom you've already formed a working relationship. They're familiar with your services and don't need to be "sold" on your expertise but they do need a subtle reminder that you care and that you'll be there when future demands arise.

For example, a thank you card or letter that conveys your appreciation for their business is a follow up that generates increased sales. Before your thank you is forgotten, a return visit or telephone call will continue your business association.

Perhaps a gift certificate to a local restaurant or the movie theater, or an item such as a coffee mug with your logo on it, is what's needed to evoke a pleasant surprise. And, after sending your client a gift, be sure to make an additional follow-up telephone call to see whether they've received it.

Secondly, don't file away all those prospective client contacts after the initial meeting. You've already laid the foundation and that's usually the most difficult element. Now build on that surface by reinforcing the strength of your advertising solutions.

Mail a card or letter thanking them for their time but continuing the sales presentation. For instance, you could say, "It was a pleasure speaking with you last Tuesday, Ms. Jones. Thank you for permitting me to share a moment of your busy schedule. I could see you were concerned with getting the best quality assistance for your mother. That's why the services we spoke about are the best quality services available. We will provide your mother with the assistance she requires while providing her with the independence she needs. Jo Ann's Home Care's main focus is providing cost effective services to you and your mother. Again thank you for allowing me to explain our services. I look forward to assisting you and your mother in the future.

Then, call back and follow up on the letter or card without delay. And when you do, remember to value their time and be brief. You don't want to leave a pesky impression prompting the client to dread your next communication. By leaving a wonderful taste in their mouths you've paved the way for another contact within 30 to 90 days. Again, a simple, yet effective step to increased sales using the follow-up approach.

So don't let the goal of increased sales slip right through your fingers! Employ a tried-and-true method, the follow up, and enjoy a simple step to boosting your bottom line.

7

One may walk over the highest mountain one step at a time.
--- **John Wanamaker**

Managing Your Day to Day Operations

Managing the Workforce Crunch

Business has never been better; a lot of new clients are coming in. If only you could get the needed help, you could really take advantage of this boom. Where are those qualified employees? Probably on someone else's payroll or even bidding against you!

Because the economy has been good for the last few years, qualified employees have been snatched away by companies willing to give an extra incentive -- be it monetary or other. In addition, trustworthy workers usually turn into entrepreneurs of their own, especially when the economic climate is favorable.

So does your Non-Medical Home Care Business have a chance at hiring adequate assistance? Are there some unexplored sources to tap into? What are some alternatives to managing that workforce crunch? Explore ideas from the obvious to the innovative. You never know where you'll find the right solution for your business.

You've probably thought of this utterly obvious solution – apprentice programs through universities and colleges. But, have you pursued it? Why haven't you? Students are willing to work part-time after school, evenings, weekends and usually any time your other employees don't want to. Work/study programs with community colleges may even be the perfect source for a future partner. Contact the school placement office for details.

Would homemakers or mothers wanting to rejoin the workforce be able to assist you? Some may have caregiving skills, office skills and other talents just waiting to be applied. Since many enjoy working when their children are in school, these potential employees could fill in most of the day and still be home early. You benefit by getting an "almost full-time" employee at a "little more than part-time" price. Most caregivers work from 10 to 20 hours per week for $8 - $12 per hour.

With years of experience in handling people, retirees can make excellent sales professionals. Studies have shown that more mature individuals show more concern for clients and display knowledge regarding how to do things for which there are no written instructions. Many Non-Medical Home Care services hire women caregivers between 40 and 65 years old, exactly what any Non-Medical Home Care business needs! Why not contact senior associations in your area?

Use an employment agency to lease qualified professionals or bright temporary help. Besides getting your business through the squeeze, the temps may even end up staying on. Of course, you'll have to pay a fee to the agency for screening and locating them for you.

Ask current employees for skilled referrals. Offer a bonus when those referrals result in a placement. That'll get them thinking! Or, find out from vendors whether they know of anyone that's looking for a permanent position. Sales reps have a large network and can also assist you in getting the word out.

> **Better Business Tip**
>
> *Know the amount of work to be done monthly in*
>
> *your company, and the number of people necessary*
>
> *to do it and hire them - the best!*

Sometimes a solution can be so obvious it's often overlooked. Have you thought of paying overtime to existing employees? Even if it's only temporary, your current crew may be able to use the extra income. What's more, the supplementary expenditure may be nothing compared to the expense of training new help.

So let the good times roll and learn how to take advantage of the economic upswing. Start managing that workforce crunch by hiring the needed help from some usual and not-so-usual places. And remember to offer that extra incentive that'll nab and retain qualified assistance. Keep your business booming along with the economy!

Understanding Employment Law

The following is a brief synopsis of some of the federal statutes governing employers that may apply to your business. Obviously, the statutes themselves are much more detailed. This list is simply a representative sampling of the potentially applicable statutes and is by no means all-inclusive. Whether or not these laws apply to your Non-Medical Home Care business may be determined by the number of employees working for you, so if your business is growing, be sure you know the rules of the road for employers. You may wish to consult with a lawyer if you want to know more about the laws that may apply to your specific business.

The number of people your business employs makes a difference in what laws apply to your business. The following laws apply no matter what size your business is:

- Fair Labor Standards Act (FLSA)

- Social Security

- Federal Insurance Contributions Act (FICA)

- Medicare

- Equal Pay Act (EPA)

- Immigration Reform and Control Act (IRCA)

- Federal Unemployment Tax Act (FUTA)

The following additional laws apply if you have more than 10 employees:

- Occupational Safety & Health Administration Act (OSHA)

The following additional laws apply if you have more than 14 employees:

- Title VII Civil Rights Act

- Americans with Disabilities Act (ADA)

- Pregnancy Discrimination Act

The following additional laws apply if you have more than 19 employees:

- Age Discrimination in Employment Act (ADEA)

- Older Worker Benefit Protection Act (OWBPA)

- Consolidated Omnibus Budget Reconciliation Act (COBRA)

The following additional laws apply if you have more than 49 employees:

- Family Medical Leave Act (FMLA)

The following additional laws apply if you have more than 99 employees:

- Worker Adjustment and Retraining Notification Act (WARN)

- Employee Retirement Income Security Act (ERISA)

Employee Registration Requirement
As an U.S. employer, you are responsible for completion and retention of Form I-9 for each individual you hire for employment in the United States. This includes citizens and non-citizens. On the form, the employer must verify the employment eligibility and identity documents presented by the employee and record the document information on the Form I-9. I-9 Forms can be obtained by downloading from the U.S. Citizenship and Immigration Service (USCIS) Website.

Equal Employment Opportunity Commission (EEOC) Requirements
When advertising for and interviewing job candidates, it's important to focus exclusively on the skill and experience needed for the position. Under Title VII of the Civil Rights Act of 1964, the Americans with Disabilities Act (ADA), and the Age Discrimination in Employment Act (ADEA), it is illegal to discriminate in any aspect of employment, including hiring; compensation, assignment, or classification of employees; job advertisements; recruitment; testing; training and apprenticeship programs; or other terms and conditions of employment. Many states and municipalities also have enacted protections against discrimination and harassment based on sexual orientation, status as a parent, marital status and political affiliation. For information, please contact the EEOC District Office nearest you.

Union Requirements
Right to Work states secure the right of employees to decide for themselves whether or not to join or financially support a union, and makes it illegal for unions to require membership as a condition of

employment. In non-Right to Work states, employees may be required to join unions in order to retain employment at some companies regardless of opposing political views or religious beliefs. If unions have or are forming in your business, find out what the law is in your state.

Reference Checks

When called for reference checks, you are generally expected to reveal only the employees' date of hire, date of termination and job title, and are prohibited from giving confidential information. If the applicant signs a "waiver and hold harmless agreement" as a condition for applying for employment, you may feel more comfortable specifying additional information specified by the agreement.

Credit Checks

To obtain a credit report on an employee or prospective employee, you must provide clear and conspicuous written notice that a credit report may be requested, and obtain written consent from the applicant or employee.

Background Checks

You generally have the right to access arrest and conviction records that are public information, but whether you can use such information for hiring decisions varies from state to state. Some states allow employers to discriminate based on criminal convictions, but not on arrests. Other states apply varying rules depending on the position or industry being applied for. Check with your State labor department to find out what laws may apply to you.

Employing Foreign Workers

If you are contemplating hiring foreign workers, be sure to review the U.S. Citizenship and Immigration Services Employment Handbook.

<u>People with Disabilities</u>
Visit the Social Security Administration's Employers' Web page for information on hiring people with disabilities, including tax incentives, referral services, FAQ's, and helpful links to the Department of Labor's Office of Disability Employment Policy.

<u>Employing Military Reservists and National Guardsmen</u>
Find out what your obligations are under the Uniformed Services Employment and Reemployment Rights Act (USERRA) by using the U.S. Department of Labor's Resource Guide to USERRA.

Conducting Interviews and Making Job Offers

Selecting caregivers can be a daunting task. Out of 200 applicants, five may be hired and only after credit, criminal background and motor vehicle checks have been performed and references verified.

So where do you start? Successful hiring begins with reviewing the job description for the position you have open. If you don't have up-to-date job descriptions, you need to create an accurate job description defining the essential duties, qualifications, physical demands, and work environment of the job.

It's important to know and understand what the job is all about. In hiring decisions, you have to be able to make a judgment, not just about the person being interviewed, but also about the fit between the person and the job.

Well-written job descriptions help you hire the right people and make the kind of fair employment decisions you can defend in court.

There are various recruiting sources available for finding the best applicants, for instances personal recommendations, internal recruitment, employee referrals, college recruiting, employment agencies, and employment ads. Depending on the size and needs of your Non-Medical Home Care service, you may use one, some, or all of these sources to find applicants.

Many Non-Medical Home Care business owners believe that employee referrals are the best way to recruit new applicants. Current employees are committed to the organization and understand the work environment. And, referrals are relatively inexpensive.

However, employment ads continue to be the most widely used recruiting source. To avoid drowning in a sea of resumes, it is important to write clear and specifically defined employment ads. Such ads will not only dissuade unqualified applicants, but will also make the recruiting process much more efficient.

Once you've gathered resumes it's time to match them with your job description to screen out unqualified applicants. Review promising resumes and make notes of or highlight areas you'd like to discuss.

It is a good idea to prepare questions in advance that you want to ask of all your applicants. Ask specific questions about areas of expertise relating to the job to test actual knowledge.

Avoid asking illegal questions that deal with the applicant's sex, race, age, marital status, disabilities, religious beliefs, national origin, and sexual preference. Such questions might be interpreted as being discriminatory. Focus on the applicant's qualifications, experience, abilities, and future goals. Below are examples of questions you <u>should not</u> ask. Note: Be on guard even when you're chatting informally.

Questions that could be considered discriminatory:

- Are you married?
- What is that accent you have?
- Where is your spouse from?
- Are you engaged?
- Do you have children?
- Where are you from?
- Were you born here?
- What is your ethnic heritage?
- What church do you go to?
- How old are you?
- When were you born?
- When did you graduate from high school?

Almost every applicant will have been coached or read about typical interview questions such as:

- Why did you leave your last job?
- Why do you want this job?
- Where do you see yourself in 5 years?
- What are your strengths? What are your weaknesses?
- What did you like most about your last job?

- What did you like least about your last job?

Those questions will certainly provide valuable information, but you may want to come up with questions for which the applicant will be less prepared. Some examples might be:

- Tell me about the best boss you ever had. Why was he/she the best?

- Tell me about the worst boss you ever had. Why was he/she the worst?

- What's the most important thing a boss can do to support you?

- How do you solve problems?

- Describe a work conflict and how you resolved it?

- What are some things your last employer could have done to be more successful?

- What area of your skills do you want to improve in the next year?

Before starting the interview be certain to make your purpose clear. Even though it may seem obvious why the person is there, you should reiterate the purpose of the interview. Without yet getting into details about the job, confirm the position that is open and briefly explain your process for conducting interviews. Is this a screening interview? Will there be others to talk to? Will there be a follow-up interview?

Give applicants an approximate length of time for the interview and check to be sure that it won't conflict with their schedule.

Explain to applicants up front that all references and work history will be checked. Ask for permission to contact current employers and for names of key players in their past work life.

It is your responsibility to use the right techniques and ask meaningful questions to get all the information needed to make a smart hiring decision. To do that, you need to keep the interview on track and focused on job-related questions.

Refer to your list of questions if necessary. Don't get caught in the common interviewing mistake of talking too much and listening too little. Encourage the applicant to do most of the talking by asking open-ended questions.

Probe for details of the applicant's competence (experience, education, aptitude), work attitudes (enthusiasm, likes, dislikes, goals), and social attitudes (personality, integrity, character). Be prepared for moments of silence. Brief periods of silence are all right and may induce additional information. Too much silence, though, can be awkward.

It is also important to listen carefully and take notes. Your purpose is to gather job-related information about the applicant. To do that you need to actively listen and pay attention to everything being said. Applicants will be more at ease and talkative if you show your undivided attention. Take brief reminder notes of key things the applicant says. You can use these notes and elaborate on them immediately after the interview. You may also want to jot down follow-up questions to issues that were raised or incidents you want to explore. Explain that you are going to take notes in advance. Write quickly and briefly to avoid distracting or disturbing the applicant.

Give the applicant time to ask questions about the job and your company. If the applicant asks meaningful and thoughtful questions, you can gain additional insight into his/her thinking process and long-term goals. Be prepared to answer tough questions such as:

- How is excellent performance rewarded?

- What are the organization's values and ethics?

- How does the organization support career development?

- How secure is the position and the organization?

Lastly the end of the interview is the appropriate time to describe in detail the essential duties of the job and how they fit into your Non-Medical Home Care service. It is also the time to talk about the organization's culture, how people and different departments interact, and what is expected of employees. Providing this information too early in the interview gives the applicant clues on how to answer your questions.
Be honest about the job and the organization. If there are negatives, bring them up and discuss them. Potential employees should have a good idea of what they are getting into and what they can expect on the job.
Discuss salary expectations, work schedule, and benefits you offered. Explain the next steps in your hiring process. Close by thanking applicants for their time and interest in your organization.

It is important that you allow yourself time after each interview to collect your thoughts and rate the applicant. This can include elaborating on the notes taken during the interview and your reflections on how the applicant answered job-related questions.
Avoid personal reactions to the applicant. Focus on the essential duties and requirements of the position. Based on the background and skills, how might the applicant perform in the position? Be prepared to justify statements that you write down.
The three most important questions you need to answer to guarantee quality hires are:

1. Is the applicant able to do the job?

2. Is the applicant willing to do the job?

3. Is the applicant manageable, once on the job?

Hiring top-quality employees is vital to your Non-Medical Home Care business. Employees are your most important resource and the greatest contributors to your success. They are a valued-asset that should be carefully selected and nurtured.

How to Keep the Top Talent

How do you attract, and then keep, your most talented people committed, loyal and motivated? The question has frustrated and even bewildered a growing number of companies in the past year or two. The work force and pool of resources of highly skilled, highly trained talent is shrinking.

This is not a new problem, but it seems to be ever more critical. The question of attracting the brightest and best is a key issue for successful companies. Today with large signing bonuses and very attractive salaries and benefits, the more perplexing question is how to best build the loyalty of our talented people. The more talent we retain, the more talent we'll attract.

Loyalty in most business generally builds over time. As a new business owner you may not have the luxury of extended time or stability to build loyalty. You have to quickly catch the attention of talent, give them an exciting vision of your company's future, and show them how they are an essential part of the success.

When people feel they are contributing to a worthwhile service, their level of commitment increases. People want to be excited about their work. Loyalty also increases when people feel respected and acknowledged for what they do. People want to feel valued and that they are making a difference. Leaders need to recognize each person's need to feel like they count.

Do you let each member on your team know how he or she fit into your company's success and ever-changing environment?

Do you know what each of your people wants and finds most important?

A recent study of exit interviews found that money was not the reason good talent was leaving. They wanted to be part of a worthwhile enterprise, be influential in decision-making, and create and contribute to mutually agreed-upon objectives.

Check your leadership effectiveness in skills needed to retain talent: Rate yourself 1-5, with 5 being outstanding.

1. Do you fully cooperate with all of your staff to find win-win solutions?
2. Do you give credit and acknowledgment without fail to those deserving?
3. Do you regularly encourage, support and contribute to your staff's success?
4. Do you often increase your staff's responsibilities and opportunities?
5. Do you frequently provide training and learning opportunities for staff?
6. Do you treat all staff with dignity and respect as you do your best client?
7. Do you encourage creativity and seek candid feedback from staff?

Top talent remains loyal when they believe there are chances for professional growth and challenge. As the business owner, you should invest more time planning for these growth opportunities. You might identify cross-functional team projects where your talent can effectively network and work with different teams.

High achievers want to be in contact and dialog with the colleagues they respect. Identify ways to bring the best minds together. Successful people relish the opportunity to learn from each other and communicate on deeper levels.

When you set your quarterly goals, try a goal alignment process. Ask your team to identify the key stakeholders who could either support or impede their progress. Facilitate some meetings with other groups to seek creative ways to align goals and develop improved solutions.

Taking time to coach and mentor your people pays off. Point out opportunities in their career growth like encouraging specific training. Don't be afraid to ask them tough questions and guide them in finding the right path. Help them identify ways to leverage their skills and accomplishments. Encourage or sponsor them for professional organizations. Give meaningful feedback on how they can get ahead and be of more value to your Non-Medical Home Care service.

Catch them doing something right. Then catch them again and again and again. The more good talent we retain, the more we will attract.

Conducting Reference Checks

Regardless of the size of your Non-Medical Home Care business, pre-employment screening is a necessary hiring practice to avoid lawsuits and costly hiring mistakes. Gone are the days of a simple reference check and a few phone calls to screen new employees. Amid security concerns, corporate scandals, and workplace violence, pre-employment screening has been gaining ground.

Pre-employment screening is the process of using psychometric testing, background checks, and drug testing to determine the background and identity of hiring a new employee. Background checking is a popular method of pre-employment screening. Over 82% of HR professionals report that their companies do background checks of new hires, up from 66% in 1996 according to The Society for Human Resource Management Workplace Violence Survey.

Before you delve right into a thorough background check of your new recruit, consider the potential legal landmines that can impact your small business. Investigating the background of a potential hire can help minimize the risk of negligent-hiring lawsuits. You and your company can be held liable for the actions of a new employee especially if you did not perform a background check.

Fair Credit Reporting Act

Prior to beginning a background check, it's important your Non-Medical Home Care business complies with the Fair Credit Reporting Act and the American With Disabilities Act. Under the FCRA, your small business is required to have employees sign a disclosure form granting authorization to perform a background check. The FCRA is not just restricted to credit reports but includes all "consumer reports." Laws will vary from state-to-state in how and what information can be used during the pre-employment screening process. For instance, your state laws may prohibit using certain aspects of a criminal record during a background check. Your state may have different laws, such as California's Investigative Consumer Reporting Agencies Act. Consult with local regulators and legal counsel before going too deep into the criminal past of a new hire.

<u>The American With Disabilities Act (ADA)</u>
Under ADA, employers are restricted in using medical or disability data in the hiring process. Simply put, you cannot ask during the interview or background check about a person's disabilities. The ADA covers businesses with 15 or more employees, including state and local governments.

Outsourcing Your Pre-Employment Screening

One solution for small businesses undertaking pre-employment screening is to employ the services of a background checking company. Hiring an outsider can help in finding accurate, complete information on job candidates. Your outsourcing partner should be able to steer you through the legal requirements as well as federal and State regulations of background screening. Another added bonus is under FCRA; your small business can have limited legal immunity by using a third-party background pre-employment screening company.

Whether your small business decides to outsource or conduct pre-employment screening practices on your own, take the necessary time to educate yourself on the process. Many small business agencies such as SCORE or the Small Business Administration (SBA) can provide counsel. Visit your government's websites on FCRA and ADA. Background screening should always be a standard practice of operating a successful Non-Medical Home Care business.

Billing Your Clients

Non-Medical Home Care companies vary in price, contract agreements and accepted form of payments. Some accept insurance, Medicare, Passport or Options, while others are self-pay.

Payment Options

Non-Medical Home Care services can be paid by a variety of public and private sources or directly by the patient or the patient's family members. You should help the client determine the appropriate payer source before initiating Non-Medical Home Care services. The following are some payment options:

- Medicare
  Medicare is an available program for most patients over the age of 65. If an individual is homebound, under a physician's care, and requires medically necessary skilled nursing, therapy services or Home Care services, he/she may be eligible for services.

- Medicaid
  Medicaid is a joint federal-state medical assistance program for low-income individuals. It is administered by the state. Most state will cover nursing, physical and occupational therapy, and Home Care services.

- PASSPORT
  PASSPORT is a Medicaid program that is provided through a special waiver from the center for Medicare and Medicaid Services (CMS). This program offers an alternative to clients who meet Medicaid Home Care and nursing home qualifications.

- Worker's Compensation
  Worker's compensation is a private third party

payer. Individuals who are ill or injured as a
result of their employment are eligible for
Worker's compensation.

- Self-Pay
  Self-pay is an option for payment of services that
  are not covered by public or private third party
  payers.

Running a Payroll System

Managing your company's payroll requires more than
simply writing out checks and paying employees on
time. Your business' payroll solution needs to manage a
vast array of record keeping and regulatory issues,
including:

- Processing and distributing paychecks each pay
  period

- Calculating state and federal employment taxes

- Filing payroll-related tax reports

- Complying with government regulations

- Managing employee paperwork and direct deposit
  details

- Tracking vacation time, sick leave, and company
  holidays

- Overseeing voluntary deductions for 401(k)
  contributions, flexible spending accounts, and
  health care plans

There are a number of ways small businesses handle these responsibilities. The task of managing your company's payroll can be delegated to a staff member, managed by your accountant, or outsourced to a payroll service provider (a company that contracts with your business to handle payroll details, including check generation, tax filings, and compliance with government regulations).

The following breakdown of each method's advantages and disadvantages can be used to help you decide which is right for your company.

Internal Management By Staff Member(s)

Advantage:

- Highest level of control over payroll issues

Disadvantages:

- Requires staff expertise in multiple areas

- Greater opportunity for error

- Company is directly liable for IRS filing errors

- Actual cost is often higher than expected due to additional man-hours invested in payroll-tax preparation and filing

- Companies often reap greater value from staff member's time being devoted to core business issues

Accountant

Advantages:

- Management by financial expert

- Offers more control than payroll service provider, less than internal staff member

Disadvantages:

- May be unable to manage payroll add-ons such as 401(k) plans and direct deposit

- Often more costly than internal management or payroll services

- May take more time to prepare payroll documents than payroll service providers

<u>Payroll Service Provider</u>

Advantages:

- Payroll expertise: these companies are familiar with all necessary tax and regulatory issues

- May be able to provide additional services such as 401(k) and direct deposit

- Controls your payroll processing costs by setting a standard fee

- May take financial responsibility for fees and penalties resulting from payroll filing errors

Disadvantages:

- Restricted opportunities to make adjustments to payroll amounts

- One step removed from tax filing documentation

The decision to outsource or not may also come down to cost. To find out which payroll management option is most affordable, estimate the number of hours you or your employees spend calculating and preparing checks, computing and filing tax forms, and preparing additional payroll documents such as W-2s or direct deposit information.

Add to this figure the time spent correcting IRS filing errors, and then multiply your total by an hourly wage that represents the value of your and your employees' time. Compare this figure to the cost of having your accountant manage payroll (based on his/her hours and fees) and to a payroll provider's fees.

Handling Your Recordkeeping

<u>Records</u>
Good records are essential. Without them your business will not know where it's been, where it is, or where it's heading. Keeping records that are accurate, up-to-date, and easy to use is one of your most important functions. Depending on the size and complexity of your Non-Medical Home Care Service, keeping accurate records can be as simple as recording transactions on a general journal and/or special journal.
 A general journal is the basic record of the business. Every monetary event in the life of your Non-Medical Home Care service is entered in the general journal or in one of the special journals.

Proper bookkeeping is important for sustaining and expanding your business. Without it, you run the risk of hitting cash flow crunches, wasting money, and missing out on opportunities to expand. When you are devising your bookkeeping routine, remember that the purpose of bookkeeping is to help you manage your business and to enable the IRS to evaluate your business activity. As long as your bookkeeping achieves both of these objectives, it can -- and should -- be as simple as possible.

The general guidelines below outline what you must take care of and also provide ideas for how to keep your books in an orderly manner. But before making any decisions regarding bookkeeping, check with your accountant or tax preparer because bookkeeping needs vary dramatically by state.

You may choose to use software to keep track of various aspects of your business, and resources are provided here to help you institute computer automation. The key to taking full advantage of bookkeeping software is to determine if it saves you time and frees you up to concentrate on running your business. In many cases it will, but be careful not to fall into the trap of wasting time setting up computer bookkeeping that could be more efficiently handled on paper. The paper bookkeeping forms mentioned here can be obtained from most stationary stores.

Some bookkeeping functions are best relegated to an accountant. While it is essential to retain a thorough knowledge by reviewing your books frequently, an accountant or bookkeeper can free you up to concentrate on expanding your business. Even a bookkeeping task that takes only a few hours a week may be better relegated to someone else if that time can be better spent.

A Revenue and Expense Journal is used by most small businesses and is single entry accounting -- recording receipts and expenditures only. Double-entry accounting involves a ledger and necessitates that each activity be recorded as a debit and a credit on your books. In the past it was thought that all businesses needed to use the more cumbersome method of double entry, but the single-entry system is now used for many small business owners. Single-entry accounting can be kept on paper or computer. Programs that perform single-entry accounting include Quicken by Intuit and Microsoft Money among many others.

If you use double-entry accounting you may want to use a computer program or a bookkeeper to keep your ledger up to date. If you allow anyone else to keep your books be sure you review them regularly. Programs that do double-entry bookkeeping include: Peachtree Accounting by Peachtree Software, and QuickBooks by Intuit.

Cash spent on your business needs to be accounted for if you want to record all business expenses in a given year. There are at least two ways to do this: write yourself reimbursable checks or keep a petty cash record.

If you choose to pay yourself back with a check, simply keep track of all cash receipts and total them weekly, biweekly or monthly, depending on your volume of expenses. Keep a log of each category of expense, for tax purposes and write yourself a check for the total. Write cash reimbursable in your check register to differentiate this from taxable income. Alternatively, you can keep a petty cash record by writing a check to petty cash and keeping a log of each expense paid out of petty cash.

If you plan on allowing your clients to pay for your Non-Medical Home Care services in arrears, then you will need an accounts receivable tracking system. Your Accounts Receivable records keep track of what is owed to you. You can monitor accounts receivable by holding on to a copy of all invoices sent out or by keeping an Accounts Receivable record. Either way, the information you need to capture includes: invoice date, invoice number, invoice amount, terms, date paid, amount paid, and the name of the entity being billed.

Many software programs are available to help you generate invoices and track hours and expenses incurred for each client. These programs can save you hours and create professional-looking invoices. Software programs that will create invoices or track hours include QuickBooks® by Intuit and Timeslips® by Peachtree Software.

Accounts payable are debts owed by your company for goods and services. Keeping track of what you owe and when it is due will enable you to establish good credit and hold onto your money as long as possible.

Business owners with few accounts payable items use accordion file folders labeled with dates to keep track. Other small businesses simply pay bills twice per month and keep all bills in a "To Pay" folder. Larger companies use accounts payable paper records organized by creditor. Regardless of the system you choose, you should retain the following information about accounts payable: invoice date, invoice number, invoice amount, terms, date paid, amount paid, balance (if applicable), and clients' names and addresses.

<u>Employees</u>
Another critical area of recordkeeping for your Non-Medical Home Care business is employee recordkeeping. As soon as you hire an employee, you must have him or her fill out a W-4 form (Employee's Withholding Allowance Certificate), which lists their name, address, social security number, marital status and the number of personal exemptions they are claiming. New employees must also sign and date the form. As the employer, you do not need to send it to the IRS, but you must keep it on file. New employees must also complete Form I-9 (Employment Eligibility Verification) for the Immigration and Naturalization Service (INS). Form I-9 must also remain on file at your place of business for possible INS inspections. The penalties for not having the INS forms are steep. All employees should have social security numbers (SSN).

Handling Taxes Issues

As a small business owner, you are responsible for a variety of taxes corporate, personal, employee, and property (at the federal, state, and sometimes local, levels). Each company has a unique tax profile depending on: type of business, number of employees, profits (or losses), corporate status, assets, and location. You should consider using a tax accountant or a professional advisor who is familiar with the requirements for your business.

<u>Corporate Income Taxes (corporations)</u>
If you have chosen to incorporate your Non-Medical Home Care business, you must file and pay federal income taxes, and, in many cases, state and local income taxes as well.

If you are a C Corporation, you will pay income taxes on income left over after business expenses. These taxes are calculated on a sliding scale that usually increases as your income rises. You may also be liable for other taxes, such as personal-holding-company taxes and the accumulated-earnings tax. You should consult with your tax advisor to see exactly what corporate income taxes apply to your company.

If you are an S Corporation, your company, in most cases, will not pay direct taxes. Instead, the income or loss is passed on directly to the shareholders, who pay the tax at the personal rate. Be aware that some states do not recognize S corporation status and tax the company directly. No matter what kind of corporation you are, your federal corporate returns are due a month prior to personal income tax returns -- the fifteenth day of the third month after the company's fiscal year ends. So, if your year ends on December 31, your tax return is due March 15, instead of April 15. Corporate estimated taxes are due on the 15th day of the fourth, sixth, ninth, and twelfth month after the end of the fiscal year. For a year ending on December 31, that would be April 15, June 15, September 15, and December 15.

<u>Personal Income Taxes (sole proprietorships, partnerships)</u>
If your Non-Medical Home Care business operates as a sole proprietorship or partnership, you must pay city, state, and federal income tax just like anyone else and you are responsible for paying it directly to the government. Federal income taxes must be paid in estimated quarterly payments. These payments are due in four installments on: April 15, June 15, September 15, and January 15. These federal taxes will cover your self-employment tax, which includes social security and Medicare. This self-employment tax makes working for yourself expensive because when you had a boss, your employer paid for half your self-employment tax and you paid the other tax. You will now be responsible for all of it, although a portion of it is deductible.

If your state has an income tax, you must pay it quarterly also. Cities may have their own tax rules.

Generally speaking, you must pay estimated quarterly installments if you expect to owe at least $500 in tax for a given year. The laws governing how much tax you must submit during the year require that you either pay 90 percent of the tax you will owe by the end of the year (to avoid penalties), or pay 100 percent of last year's tax (110% if your income exceeds $150K). This means that you can submit a minimum amount of tax during the year if you want to hold on to some of your money. However, this plan only works if you are able to leave the money intended for taxes alone. Too many people spend the money that they put aside then run into trouble at tax time. If you fail to make your payments on schedule and within these guidelines, you will be liable for penalties -- plus interest on the money you owe.

Your tax preparer should provide you with forms and envelopes for making your estimated payments, or you can order these forms directly from the IRS by calling 800-829-3676.

Employment Taxes
If you have employees on your payroll, your tax situation is significantly more complex. You'll have to keep track of payroll taxes, employee withholding, Social Security, Medicare, unemployment, disability, and worker's comp, to name a few. All of these require separate calculations and timelines for payment. These rules are very strict and complex, and if you're not in the payroll business, hire an accountant or a payroll service to keep yourself legal and punctual with all these payments.

As mentioned in an earlier section, all employees must fill out a federal W-4 form and a Form I-9 from the Immigration and Naturalization Service. You should also check with your state's office of taxation to find out about state income tax, unemployment, and worker's compensation, as well as what forms, if any, need to be filed.

With your first employee you become responsible for filing forms and paying payroll taxes, including the following:

- Withholding - Social Security (FICA), Medicare tax, federal and state income taxes are withheld from your employees' pay.

- Employer Matching - Employers must match the FICA and Medicare taxes and pay it along with the employees' share.

- Unemployment - These include both federal unemployment taxes (FUTA) as well as state unemployment tax (SUTA).

- Worker's Compensation - Although not a tax, worker's comp is often handled along with other taxes by a bookkeeper or accountant.

The only way to avoid employee taxes is to hire workers as independent contractors. Note: this usually does not work well in the Non-Medical Home Care industry. If you choose to hire independent contractor, remember that there are strict IRS rules designed to keep employers from using the classification as a way to avoid paying employee taxes. In general, to qualify as an independent contractor, a worker must work for other people and complete tasks with his or her own tools or equipment. Check with your accountant before classifying anyone as an independent contractor. If you hire an independent contractor and pay that person more than $600 during the year, you must issue them a 1099 Form, reporting the name, address and social security number or EIN (employer identification number) of the recipient and the amount paid to that person for the calendar year. The Form 1099 reports to the government that this person was paid as a non-employee. This gives you the right to deduct those payments as an expense and tells the IRS to look for that money as income on your non-employee's Schedule C form. Your tax preparer should provide you with forms and envelopes for making your estimated payments, or you can order these forms directly from the IRS by calling 800-829-3676.

Sales Tax

A state sales tax ID number is basically a business version of your Social Security number under which you collect and pay tax for the service you sell that qualifies for taxation in your state. The state department of taxation provides sales tax ID numbers and it takes about a month to get one. The rule of thumb for sales tax is that most Non-Medical Home Care services are exempt, but you should verify this with your state's department of taxation.

Property Taxes

If your Non-Medical Home Care business owns any real estate, you will be required to pay property taxes. In addition, many commercial leases are written so that the lessor, not the lessee, is responsible for real estate taxes. Review your lease to determine who is responsible for your taxes.

Your property tax rate will be based on the assessed value of your real estate. Be aware that in many areas, commercial property is assessed at a higher level than residential property. If you believe your tax assessment is too high, you might want to consult with your attorney to file a request for a new assessment.

In addition, you might also be liable for "personal property taxes" on the estimated value of other property your company owns, such as inventory, furniture and fixtures, automobiles and trucks, etc.

<u>Ways to Pay Less in Tax</u>
Small business owners face unique tax issues. Here are some ideas to help you get the most from your business deductions, avoid problems and plan for the future.

- **Keep good books and records for your business. Keep these records separate from records of your personal expenses.**

  Keep your business records as long as necessary. Generally, this is three years after the date you filed your income tax return. However, in some cases, it's a good idea to keep records even longer. Keep detailed depreciation records for as long as you own business property. You'll need them not only to figure your current-year depreciation deduction but also to figure your basis when you sell or otherwise dispose of the property.

- **If you need to hire employees for your business, consider employing family members.**

  This will allow you to shift income to members in lower tax brackets as long as they provide bona fide services to the business. (Depending on earnings, there may be no tax at all on wages paid to the child.) You also avoid the employer share of FICA on wages to your child under age 18. And you can set up a fully deductible health insurance plan if your spouse is your employee (since the plan will cover employees and their spouses -- that's you).

- **If you need to hire employees for your business and don't have any suitable family members, consider hiring workers who will**

give you a special tax benefit.

Hiring certain workers entitles you to claim a tax credit (work opportunity credit, empowerment zone credit, or Indian employment credit). Before advertising for help, check with your state employment agency on whether it can assist you in getting workers who will entitle you to a tax credit.

- **Use the standard mileage rate to deduct your car expenses as a way of simplifying your record keeping if you are eligible to use this rate.**

But if you have all receipts to show your car expenses, figure your deduction using the standard mileage rate and the actual expense method; then choose the method that gives you the greater deduction. In either case, be sure to keep track of the dates, mileage, and purpose of your automobile use.

- **Keep records to substantiate your travel and entertainment expenses.**

While you don't have to keep receipts for expenses (other than lodging) of $75 or less, you must still note in a log or diary the business purpose for the expense, the date it was incurred, and the amount you spent.

- **Plan equipment purchases carefully to get the most from your depreciation deductions.**

Because of conventions, the timing of your purchase can affect the amount of depreciation you can deduct. Or you may be able to expense up to $100,000 of the cost of equipment as long as you begin to use it by the last day of the year.

- **Use retirement plans not only to save for your retirement needs but also to reduce current taxes.**

  If you have not yet set up a retirement plan, consider a Keogh, SEP or SIMPLE plan to put more away on a tax-deductible basis than you can under an IRA. But if the tax year has closed and you haven't set up a Keogh, then look to the other plans, which allow you to set them up and make contributions until the due date of your return (including extensions) that will be deductible for the prior year. For example, if you receive a four-month filing extension, you can set up a SEP and fund it for 2005 as late as August 15, 2006.

- **If you have a sideline business that shows a loss, make sure you run it in a businesslike way, in order to prove your profit motive (so your loss will be deductible).**

  Keep separate books, records and business bank accounts. Change business operations with an eye toward making a profit.

- **File your income tax return on time or obtain a filing extension.**

  If you don't, you risk interest and penalties for late filing. You also lose the opportunity to make certain tax elections required to be made on a timely filed return.

- **If your business suffered a loss, get the most benefit from a net operating loss.**

Carry back the loss to generate an immediate tax refund. Or, if you anticipate greater profits in the future that will put you into a higher tax bracket, consider waiving the net operating loss carryback and carrying your loss forward to the next year.

Employee Training -- A Wise Investment for Non-Medical Home Care Providers

Increasingly local competition and our changing economy are reasons why Home Care professionals have looked to employee training as a wise investment – an investment that pays off in financial success and sustained growth. More and more entrepreneurs have taken the savvy approach of training their associates in not only basic business skills, but in industry-specific tasks. And, they're setting up effective programs to do so.

Whether it's one of the Non-Medical Home Care industry's largest companies or small establishments that are just around the corner, all have had to work with the resources at hand and within their budgets. From the millions lavished to just a few dollars spent, all have seen fruitage from their efforts. The most important thing they did was start. So, how can you benefit from their example?

Start small and start today. Begin an in-house program where seasoned employees show recent hires new skills. This one-on-one interaction builds team spirit as well. Don't reason that you'll put off implementing training until things settle down. As you know, they probably never will! Since experienced workers know all the particular quirks of your business, they're your best teachers.

Use books, tapes, and videos. What an inexpensive educational program! There are training aids that cover everything from marketing to organization. In the Non-Medical Home Care arena, industry-specific media is available that covers a broad range of topics from dealing with state agencies to legal issues you should know. It is a great idea to maintain a library of resource materials. You might want to consider having

- First Aid

- CPR

- Injury prevention

- Nurturing care

- Security

- Dieting and meal preparation

Why not ask employees to fill out a little questionnaire after they have completed reading or viewing the material to let you know if they understand what they're learning?

Send them to school. Try some of the seminars and classes offered at industry trade shows or meetings. There they can receive hands-on training in focused areas. It may be a course of continuing education or it may a class on CPR. The Red Cross offer courses that might be very useful for you and your personnel.
Either way, the inexpensive investment will pay for itself many times over through increased enlightenment and productivity.

So train your associates well and reap the benefits of a knowledgeable staff. Educational programs are wise ventures that can fortify your business to handle economic fluctuations and increased competition. Start now.

8

The world has the habit of making room for the man whose actions show that he knows where he is going.
--- **Napoleon Hill**

Managing Client Services

One strategy for success in your Non-Medical Home Care business is to provide valuable client service through effective client management. To successfully introduce consistent client service you should examine your business' sales process from a client's perspective. You should monitor and manage each personal interaction and the physical surroundings and processes of your business activities to ensure your client service is meeting the changing needs and expectations of your clients.

Why Focus on Client Service?

The Non-Medical Home Care marketplace is becoming increasingly competitive, providing clients with more choices. Clients base their purchase decisions on the service they receive as well as price, quality and availability. By providing superior client service in today's business environment you are on the road to maintaining a healthy client base.

> ***Better Business Tip***
> *Go to any amount of trouble for all of your clients. Don't treat "big" or "small" clients any differently. Client referrals are powerful and a client who feels confident that you've gone out of your way to help them with a small matter is very likely to know someone who'd fit into your "big and best" client category.*

Superior Client Service is About Exceeding Client Expectations

Unfortunately a bad client service experience is shared with around 10 other people who are most likely to tell another 10 people. Superior client service is service that exceeds your client's expectations and will make your business stand out from your competitors. Satisfied clients may be motivated to return and use your services. Clients that are extremely impressed with your service are also likely to talk about your business to others. Word-of-mouth advertising is the most effective form of advertising. It costs nothing and is very valuable as it details personal experiences and has high credibility. You should review your client service strategies and plan to impress your clients.

How to Know Your Clients' Needs

Your Non-Medical Home Care business is in existence primarily due to your clients. Therefore, it is important that you understand their needs.

You may start to learn more about your clients by:

- Regularly asking your clients about the services of your business.

- Providing feedback forms for your clients to complete.

- Phoning or visiting your clients asking if your service has met their needs.

- Welcoming any client complaints and managing these complaints to avoid negative word-of-mouth.

- Keeping a list of client complaints to identify any patterns and the cause of dissatisfaction.

- Learning what your competitors are doing and why their clients are satisfied.

Client feedback is most effective when:

- You hear both positive and negative experiences.

- You regularly obtain feedback.

- The feedback is focused on what the client wants and doesn't want.

Remember that everyone in your business needs to understand your clients.

Identify Your Key Service Activities

Client service is an ongoing process. Your clients may contact you on several occasions and in various forms of communication. Each personal interaction conveys an opportunity to impress your clients and create a decisive impact on the client's perception of your business. You should identify all your key service activities and note how you meet or exceed your clients' expectations at each stage.

Some key service activities in your Non-Medical Home Care business may include:

- Responding to phone calls.

- Providing Non-Medical Home Care service information.

- Discussing service requirements.

- Sending follow-up documentation (for example to confirm contract).

- Billing (invoicing) and managing payments.

- Visiting the client.

- Handling client complaints.

- Providing follow-up calls or meetings.

Provide a Superior Service that Results in Client Satisfaction

In order to provide superior client service, your business should demonstrate client-focused qualities.

Some key qualities that contribute to superior client service are:

- **Complete Client Experience** - Make sure that your clients' needs are met.

- **Reliable Service** – Ensure your employees are on time and that they deliver your services as requested. Your clients do not want excuses - they want your excellent service.

- **Accountability** - You are responsible for providing high-quality Non-Medical Home Care services. Make sure you honor guarantees on your services.

- **Efficiency** - Deliver your service with minimum hassle for your clients.

- **Assurance** - Make sure you express courtesy and knowledge of the Non-Medical Home Care business clients must have confidence in you and be able to trust your word.

- **Attention to Details** - Make sure you attend to details. Show that you care and that you are prepared to provide individual attention to every client.

- **Appearance** - Take a look at your office from the point of view of a new client. Does this reflect the qualities of your business? What about the appearance of your employees? It is essential that you ensure everyone you employ dress professionally at all times.

Also make sure you keep in touch with your clients:

- Call your clients to check on their level of satisfaction with your service.

- Send your clients notices of forthcoming events or extended services.

- Mail your clients thank you notes/cards.

Making Client Service Your Key Competitive Advantage

Managing a client service culture in your business will make it easier to keep a high standard of client service.

Include client service as a key competitive advantage in your business. For instance, you may:

- Incorporate your client focus strategies into your business and action plans.

- Develop a business vision/mission that reflects your client focus culture.

- Have the commitment from everyone in your business to share your vision.

- Encourage a client-focused business culture in your day-to-day activities.

- Employ staff that is motivated to provide superior client service.

- Promote your vision on your letterhead, business cards, invoices and packaging. Let your clients know your vision - you'll be surprised at how they respond.

Managing Your Client Cases

The first step to managing your client's case is performing an assessment. You as the Non-Medical Home Care service provider should visit the client to discuss their situation and their home care needs. Together, with the client you should develop a care plan. You should stay in contact with the client so that necessary adjustments can be made to the care plan in the event the client's home care needs change. A key part of the care plan is the client's record.

The type of information you should include in the client record could be anything pertaining, but not limited to the items listed below.

- Medication intakes

- Name of physician

- Hospital preference

- Incidence reporting

- Family contacts

- Medical history

- Allergies

- Weaknesses

- Strengths

- Preferences

- Injuries

- Diseases

Another useful type of reporting is a book to record comments of staff on each client at the end of each shift.

Conducting Need Assessments and Care Planning

To give good care, your Non-Medical Home Care staff must assess and plan care to support each resident's life-long patterns, current interest, strengths and needs. Resident and family involvement in the care planning will give the staff information needed in order to insure that the resident gets good care.

<u>Assessment</u>
The Assessments gather information about how well clients can take care of themselves. This includes assessing when help may be needed in functional abilities (walking, eating, dressing, bathing, seeing, hearing, communication, understanding and remembering). The Assessments will allow your staff to know about a client's habits, activities and relationships in order to help the client live more comfortably.

The assessment will also help your staff when trying to solve difficulties. An example of when a good assessment helps would be when a client begins to have poor balance. This could be the result of medications, sitting too much, weak muscles, or poor fitting shoes etc. Your Non-Medical Home Care staff must know the cause in order to assist the client and to figure out the cause is much easier with a good assessment.

Assessments must be done before assigning your employee and at least once a year. Reviews should be held every three (3) months and when a client's condition changes. Remember, you are operating a Non-Medical Home Care service. Your staff should not attempt to render medical care that they are not licensed or qualified to provide.

<u>Plan of Care</u>
A plan of care is a strategy for how your staff will help your clients every day and addresses non-medical issues. This plan of care says what your staff will do and when it will happen (e.g., a Non-Medical Home Care assistant will help the client with walking to build strength). Care plans must be reviewed regularly to make sure they work and must be revised as needed. For care plans to work, clients must feel they meet their needs and must be comfortable with them.

You or your staff must conduct a care planning conference. A care planning conference is a meeting where your staff and a client and/or family members talk about daily activities, including meals, personal schedules, medical care and emotional needs. Clients and family members can talk about problems, ask questions and offer information to help your staff provide better care. It is important that all staff who work with a client be involved in the conference.

A good care plan should be specific to each client and should be written so that everyone can understand it. The plan should also reflect the client's concerns and support their well-being.

<u>Incidence Reporting/Emergency Situations</u>
You will need to determine the appropriate authorities
to contact in case of an accident. You will also need to
create your own emergency plan and will have to ensure
that all your employees know all the procedures in case
of emergency.

The Non-Medical Home Care assistant plays a crucial
role, during emergencies. The client will take his cues
from them. If they panic or exhibit distress, it is likely to
make the client even more fearful. It is imperative that
they be calm and composed. If you provide 24-hr
service, it is important to remember that many disease
symptoms tend to aggravate at night. It is wise for you
employees to remain dressed in their street clothes,
even at night. This way, any time loss or hesitancy in
taking immediate action, is minimized. You should also
ask your client to keep bathroom doors unlocked. This
is a place where many incidents can occur. Accidents,
like slipping, are commonplace here. Further, is the
added risk that comes about due to the physiological
changes associated with passing of urine/stools,
vomiting or bathing? A locked door may stand between
life and death, if a client requiring aid, cannot be
reached in time.

9

The man who makes no mistakes does not usually make anything.

--- **Edward John Phelps**

Re-evaluation of Your Business

How Is Your Business Doing?

This is a question you should ask yourself frequently. Hopefully the answers will be that you are successful and growing. But on occasion all businesses experience a downturn in their business. In an effort to prevent or lessen the impact of a downturn you should constantly re-evaluate your businesses operations.

The best way to improve your operations is to put yourself in the shoes of a potential client. You should go through every aspect of your operation with great care, thinking only as a potential client. You might consider doing this together with outside counsel, possibly your accountant. It is very difficult to look upon your "baby" without any prejudice, but try it.

If you have been honest with yourself, you can then put into place all the ideas that you thought of as a potential client. This will prove to be a very valuable exercise, and certainly an interesting eye-opener. The benefits that your business will realize as a consequence of this study can make this effort more than worthwhile and may also help you locate some new disciplines that could help you to further diversify.

Does My Image Need An Overhaul?

One of the most significant ways a business projects an image is by the way it is literally "seen". That loved but lived-in, comfortable-as-an-old-shoe perception of your Non-Medical Home Care Business may have the opposite impact if your clients are receiving an entirely different impression. Your business' organization and tidiness may need reevaluation if a client's initial panorama is anything but positive. That brings us to a question you may need to ask yourself, "Does my image need an overhaul?"

One way to determine whether your image and place of occupation need an overhaul is if clients are heard whispering, "I just can't believe she's in the Home Care business!" A better way to assess the need for changes is to ask an honest business-minded friend to evaluate your presence and be prepared for some eye-opening advice!

Sometimes it's easy to overlook the minor details that can detract from a successful image. Cleanliness and orderliness may not be your specialty! Unfortunately your client views things from a different perspective and that perspective may be the difference between winning their business and never hearing from them again. Get the point?

You should also give attention to your office exterior. May sure all burned out bulbs are replaced and signs are working properly. Especially give the exterior of your building a fresh facelift if your sign directly attaches to a wall.

Even if your office location is not a prime one, having professional-looking identification sign is an advertisement in itself. And don't forget, your vehicles are moving billboards that promote your business, too. Keep all in tip-top shape.

In addition, a few simple things such as keeping the grass maintained, the shrubbery trimmed, and the parking lot debris-free enhance your image without saying a word. Your exterior effect is an area of visual influence that can be a positive one.

Once off the highway and inside your office, your client's attention gets directed to the small stuff. Disregarding some seemingly minor areas can prove to be disastrous to closing that sale. Inadequate lighting, filmy windows, and dated waiting room seating may be interpreted as an inability to deliver professional Non-Medical Home Care services. Rate yourself as to whether cigarette smoke reeks from your office or whether the crumbs from yesterday's lunch still remain on the counter. Do you hope your clients don't look up and see the cobwebs and stained ceiling tiles precariously hanging over their heads? Are unsightly piles paperwork taking up needed space or are there (heaven help you) telephone numbers penciled onto the wall?

A deficiency in some of these areas may seem humorous but the competitive market today is no laughing matter. Once a potential client obtains the "inside" scoop, they may be gone forever. Yes, gone forever to your competitor across town!

So take care of first things first. Inside or out, take the necessary steps to overhaul your image to make sure your client "sees" you at your very best. Having the most knowledgeable and friendly staff will not help your profit margin if that client is being lost because of a negative impression. Remember, a basic avenue of generating additional revenue is already working either for or against you. It's your image.

Beating Your New Competition

Suddenly and swiftly, you're not the only kid on the block offering Non-Medical Home Care services. Hey, what happened? Where did all that new competition come from?

With all that new competition out there, it seems as if you may have to settle for a smaller piece of the pie. Right? Wrong! Don't psych yourself out with a self-defeating conclusion such as this. There's really more here than meets the eye.

Besides, do you want your clients going elsewhere and employing yet another business to get the Non-Medical Home Care services they needs. Likely not. Don't let those profits literally walk away. Consider how you can keep them!

Are you wondering whether you know the Non-Medical Home Care industry well enough? Do you feel some facets of your business need a little eye-opening education? Are you aware of the latest best practices available in the Non-Medical Home Care industry? What about your employees? Do they have access to and make use of continually advancing knowledge?

Answers to questions such as these may make the difference between a business' success and failure in today's competitive environment. The competitive edge may soon be defined in terms of how well an individual or an organization acquires and applies knowledge. Making decisions that enable your business to win depends on gaining and continuing to gain relevant information.

Better Business Tip

Don't rest on laurels. Force change. Look for things to do more efficiently or how to improve your service. Constantly evaluate your competitors, and benchmark yourself against them.

Acquiring new information about the to effectively operate your Non-Medical Home Care business is key. The informed Non-Medical Home Care Service gains practical knowledge of this by attending trade shows as well as by reading industry journals or magazines. Don't overlook hands-on training seminars offered by trade show exhibitors, and government agencies. These sources assist your business to receive vital information right from the "horse's mouth".

Make sure your employees have access too and make use of continually advancing practical information as well. Could they benefit from attendance at seminars and trade shows, too? And, especially in the area of customer service, insist they know the importance of treating potential clients with respect and fairness. A wealth of material on improving customer relation's lies as close as your local library or bookstore. Help your employees generate positive word-of-mouth marketing through their use of that knowledge for a competitive edge.

Your up-to-date awareness and implementation of marketing avenues and techniques will translate into business growth. The success of a business relies on the use of relevant information to formulate an advertising campaign that works. Insightful ideas can be found through the scanning of magazines, trade journals, and books. Valuable advertising suggestions are available at seminars as well as through the use of professional services.

Since the difference between a business' success or failure in today's competitive environment depends upon how well an individual or an organization acquires and applies information, make sure your organization gets what it needs to know and uses it as well. Remember, the competitive edge can be summed up in just a word -- knowledge.

Glossary of Terms

Accounts Payable
This represents what a business owes to its suppliers and other creditors at a given point in time.

Accounting Period
A period of time, (month, quarter, year), for which a financial statement is produced.

Acid Test

A stern measure of a company's ability to pay its short-term debts (liquid assets/current liabilities) also referred to as the Quick Ratio.

Accrual Accounting
A method of bookkeeping in which income and expenses are allocated to periods to which they apply, regardless of when actually received or paid. For example, when an invoice is rendered, its value is added to income immediately, even though it has not been paid.

Assets

Anything owned by the company having a monetary value; e.g. 'fixed' assets like buildings, plant and machinery, vehicles (these are not assets if rented and not owned) and potentially including intangibles like trademarks and brand names, and 'current' assets, such as stock, debtors and cash.

Asset Turnover

Measure of operational efficiency - shows how much revenue is produced per dollar of assets available to the business. (Sales revenue/total assets less current liabilities)

Accounts Receivable

This represents the amount due to a business by its customers at a given point in time.

Balance Sheet

Financial statement showing assets and liabilities at a specific time.

Budget

In a financial planning context the word 'budget' (as a noun) strictly speaking means an amount of money that is planned to spend on a particularly activity or resource, usually over a financial year. The verb forms are also used, meaning the act of calculating the budget or forecast.

Cash Accounting

The simplest form of accounting in which income is considered earned when received and expenses are not taken into account until paid.

Cashflow

The movement of cash in and out of a business from day-to-day direct trading and other non-trading or indirect effects, such as capital expenditure, tax and dividend payments.

Cashflow Statement

The cashflow statement provides a third perspective alongside the Profit and Loss account and Balance Sheet. The Cashflow statement shows the movement and availability of cash through and to the business over a given period, certainly for a financial year, and often also monthly and cumulatively.

Cost Of Debt Ratio (average cost of debt ratio)

Despite the different variations used for this term (cost of debt, cost of debt ratio, average cost of debt ratio, etc) the term normally and simply refers to the interest expense over a given period as a percentage of the average outstanding debt over the same period, i.e. cost of interest divided by average outstanding debt.

Cost Of Sales (COS)

Cost of sales is the value, at cost, of the goods or services sold during the period in question, usually the financial year, as shown in a Profit and Loss Account (P&L). In all accounts, particularly the P&L it's important that costs are attributed reliably to the relevant revenues, or the report is distorted and potentially meaningless.

Current Assets

Cash and anything that is expected to be converted into cash within twelve months of the balance sheet date.

Current Ratio

The relationship between current assets and current liabilities, indicating the liquidity of a business, i.e. its ability to meet its short-term obligations. Also referred to as the Liquidity Ratio.

Current Liabilities

Money owed by the business that is generally due for payment within 12 months of balance sheet date. Examples: creditors, bank overdraft, taxation.

Depreciation
Decrease in the value of equipment over time. Depreciation of equipment used for business is a tax-deductible expense.

Earnings Before Taxes

There are several 'Earnings Before ratios and acronyms: EBT = Earnings Before Taxes; EBIT = Earnings Before Interest and Taxes; EBIAT = Earnings Before Interest after Taxes; EBITD = Earnings Before Interest, Taxes and Depreciation; and EBITDA = Earnings Before Interest, Taxes, Depreciation, and Amortization. (Earnings = operating and non-operating profits (e.g. interest, dividends received from other investments). Depreciation is the non-cash charge to the balance sheet, which is made in writing off an asset over a period. Amortisation is the payment of a loan in instalments.

Employer Identification Number (EIN)

A number obtained by a business from the IRS by filing form SS-4. If you are a sole proprietorship, your EIN is your social security number.

Entrepreneur

Someone who is willing to assume the responsibility, risk and rewards of starting and operating a business.

Equipment Leases

Leases allowing companies to purchase

Fiscal Year

Any 12-month period used by a company or government as an accounting period.

Fixed Assets

Assets held for use by the business rather than for sale or conversion into cash, e.g., fixtures and fittings, equipment, buildings.

Fixed Cost

A production cost, which does not vary significantly with the volume of output. An example would be administrative costs.

Forecast

See 'budget' above.

Gross Profit

Sales less cost of goods or services sold. Also referred to as gross profit margin, or gross profit, and often abbreviated to simply 'margin'. See also 'net profit'.

Liabilities

General term for what the business owes. Liabilities are long-term loans of the type used to finance the business and short-term debts or money owing as a result of trading activities to date. Long-term liabilities, along with Share Capital and Reserves make up one side of the balance sheet equation showing where the money came from. The other side of the balance sheet will show Current Liabilities along with various Assets, showing where the money is now.

Liquidity Ratio

Indicates the company's ability to pay its short-term debts, by measuring the relationship between current assets (i.e. those which can be turned into cash) against the short-term debt value. (Current assets/current liabilities) Also referred to as the Current Ratio.

Net Assets (also called total net assets)

Total assets (fixed and current) less current liabilities and long-term liabilities that have not been capitalized (e.g., short-term loans).

Net Current Assets

Current Assets less Current Liabilities.

Net Profit

Net profit can mean different things so it always needs clarifying. Net strictly means 'after all deductions' (as opposed to just certain deductions used to arrive at a gross profit or margin). Net profit normally refers to profit after deduction of all operating expenses, notably after deduction of fixed costs or fixed overheads. This contrasts with the term 'gross profit' which normally refers to the difference between sales and direct cost of product or service sold (also referred to as gross margin or gross profit margin) and certainly before the deduction of operating costs or overheads. Net profit normally refers to the profit figure before deduction of tax, in which case the term is often extended to 'net profit before tax' or PBT.

Overhead

An expense that cannot be attributed to any one single part of the company's activities.

Profit and Loss Account (P&L)

A listing of income, expenses, and the resulting net profit or loss. This is also called an income statement.

Quick Ratio

Same as the Acid Test. The relationship between current assets readily convertible into cash (usually current assets less stock) and current liabilities. A sterner test of liquidity.

Reserves

The accumulated and retained difference between profits and losses year on year since the company's formation.

Return On Investment

Another fundamental financial and business performance measure. This term means different things to different people (often depending on perspective and what is actually being judged) so it's important to clarify understanding if interpretation has serious implications. Many business managers and owners use the term in a general sense as a means of assessing the merit of an investment or business decision. 'Return' generally means profit before tax, but clarify this with the person using the term - profit depends on various circumstances, not least the accounting conventions used in the business. In this sense most CEO's and business owners regard ROI as the ultimate measure of any business or any business proposition, after all it's what most business is aimed at producing - maximum return on investment, otherwise you might as well put your money in a bank savings account. Strictly speaking Return On Investment is defined as: Profits derived as a proportion of and directly attributable to cost or 'book value' of an asset, liability or activity, net of depreciation. In simple terms this the profit made from an investment. The 'investment' could be the value of a whole business (in which case the value is generally regarded as the company's total assets minus intangible assets, such as goodwill, trademarks, etc and liabilities, such as debt.

SBA Loan

Loans to small businesses unable to secure financing on reasonable terms through normal lending channels. The program operates through private-sector lenders that provide loans, which are guaranteed by the Small Business Administration (SBA) -- the SBA has no funds for direct lending or grants.

SBC (Small Business Centers)

These 12 GSA centers located throughout the United States can help you tap the multi-billion-dollar GSA "market" for goods and services. Contact a center nearest you.

SBDC

Small Business Development Centers are are located throughout the United States and are administered by the SBA. They provide management assistance to entrepreneurs and new business owners.

SBIC (Small Business Investment Corporation)

The SBA licenses SBICs as federally funded private venture capital firms. Money is available to small businesses under a variety of agreements.

SCORE

The Service Corps of Retired Executives is a volunteer management assistance program of the SBA. SCORE volunteers provide one-on-one counseling and workshops and seminars for small businesses. There are hundreds of SCORE offices throughout the United States.

SIC (Standard Industrial Classification Code)
A four-digit number assigned to identify a business
based on the type of business or trade involved. The
first two digits correspond to major groups such as
construction and manufacturing, while the last two
digits correspond to subgroups such as constructing
homes versus constructing highways. A business can
determine its SIC number by looking it up in a directory
published by the Department of Commerce, or by
checking in the SIC book in the reference section of a
local library. SBA size standards are based on SIC
codes.

Sole Proprietorship
The simplest (and most popular) form of business
organization. The individual is personally liable for all
debts of the business to the full extent of his or her
property. On the other hand, the owner has complete
control of the business.

Tax Number
A number assigned to a business that enables the
business to buy wholesale without paying sales tax on
goods and products. Contact your local courthouse for
additional information.

Variable Cost
Any costs which change significantly with the level of
output. The obvious example is cost of materials.

Working Capital

Current assets less current liabilities, representing the
required investment, continually circulating, to finance
stock, debtors, and work in progress.

Appendix I

Banks that are small business friendly

Alabama

Community Bank,

(205)429-1000

Peoples Community Bank,

(334)696-4431

West Alabama Bank & Trust,

www.wabt.com,

(205)375-6261

Alaska

National Bank of Alaska,

www.nationalbankofalaska.com,

(907)267-5700

First Bank,

(907)228-4218

Arizona

Community Bank of Arizona,

(520)684-7884

County Bank,

(520)771-8100

Mohave State Bank,

www.mohavestbank.com,

(520)855-0000

Arkansas

First State Bank,

www.fsbmybank.com,

(501)272-4221

Bank of Yellville,

www.bankofyellville.com,

(870)449-4231

Malvern National Bank,

www.onemoneyplace.com,

(501)332-6955

California

California Center Bank,

www.calcenterbank.com,

(213)386-2222

El Dorado Bank,

www.eldoradobank.com,

(949)830-7440

Wilshire State Bank,

www.wilshirebank.com,

(213)387-3200

Colorado

First Community Industrial Bank,

(303)399-3400

Bank of Grand Junction,

www.bogj.com,

(970)241-9000

Castle Rock Bank,

www.castlerockbank.com,

(303)688-5191

Connecticut

Webster Bank (formerly Equity Bank),

(860)571-7200

North American Bank & Trust,

www.northamericanbank.com,

(203)377-0732

Delaware

Citibank Delaware,

www.citicorp.com,

(302)323-3900

Bank of Delmarva N.A.,

www.bankofdelmarva.com,

(302)629-2700

<u>District of Columbia</u>

National Capital Bank of Washington,

(202)546-8000

First Liberty National Bank,

(202)331-7031

<u>Florida</u>

Farmers & Merchants Bank,

www.fmbbank.com,

(850)997-2591

Fidelity Bank of Florida,

(321)452-0011

First National Bank of Wauchula,

(941)773-4136

<u>Georgia</u>

Bank of Gray,

(912)986-3157

First State Bank,

(770)474-7293

Citizens State Bank of Taylor County (formerly South Georgia Community Bank),

(912)847-3465

Hawaii

Hawaii National Bank,

(808)528-7755

City Bank,

www.citybankhi.com,

(808)546-3909

Idaho

DL. Evans Bank,

www.dlevans.com,

(208)678-9076

Panhandle State Bank,

www.panhandlebank.com,

(208)263-0505

Illinois

Bank of Edwardsville,

www.4thebank.com,

(618)656-0057

Peoples National Bank of Kewanee,

www.pnb-kewanee.com,

(309)853-3333

Town & Country Bank,

(217)787-3100

Indiana

First Community Bank & Trust Co.,

(317)422-5171

First State Bank,

(812)443-4481

Scott County State Bank,

(812)752-4501

Iowa

Farmers Savings Bank,

(319)656-2265

Security Bank,

www.securitybank-decorah.com,

(319)382-9661

Bank Iowa,

(712)623-6960

Kansas

First National Bank of Conway Springs,

(316)456-2255

Rose Hill State Bank,

(316)776-2131

State Bank of Colwich,

(316)796-1221

Kentucky

Bank of Mt. Vernon,

www.bankmv.com,

(606)256-5141

Commonwealth Bank & Trust Co.,

www.cbandt.com,

(502)244-7700

Peoples Bank & Trust Co. of Hazard,

(606)436-2161

Louisiana

First Republic Bank,

www.flrstrepbank.com,

(318)728-4423

Community Trust Bank,

www.ctb-bank.com,

(318)768-2531

Peoples State Bank,

www.psbfln.com,

(318)256-2071

Maine

United Bank,

www.unitedklngfleld.com,

(207)942-5263

Union Trust Co.,

www.unlontrust.com,

(207)667-2504

Maryland

Maryland Permanent Bank & Trust Co.,

(410)356-4411

My Bank/First United (formerly First United National Bank & Trust),

www.mybankfirstunlted.com,

(301)334-3741

Peoples Bank of Kent County,

www.pbkc.com,

(410)778-3500

Massachusetts

Enterprise Bank & Trust Co.,

www.ebte.com,

(978)459-9000

Bank of Western Massachusetts,

www.bankwmass.com,

(413)781-2265

Gloucester Bank & Trust Co.,

www.gloucester.com,

(978)281-6270

Michigan

First State Bank of East Detroit,

www.thefsb.com,

(810)775-5000

First Community Bank,

www.firstcb.com,

(231)526-2114

Minnesota

Citizens State Bank,

(507)375-3201

United Community Bank,

(218)346-5700

Farmers State Bank of Madelia,

www.madelia.com,

(507)642-3251

Mississippi

First State Bank,

www.firststatebnk.com,

(601)735-1752

Omni Bank,

(662)456-5341

First Bank,

www.firstbankms.com,

(601)684-2231

Missouri

Kearney Trust Co.,

www.kearneytrust.com,

(816)628-6666

Peoples Bank,

www.peoplesbk.com,

(573)885-2511

United Bank of Union,

www.unitedbankofunion.com,

(636)583-2555

Montana

First State Bank,

www.fsbtf.com,

(406)827-3565

First Citizens Bank of Butte,

(406)494-4400

Nebraska

Dakota County State Bank,

www.dcsb.com,

(402)494-4215

Valley Bank & Trust,

(308)632-7500

Platte Valley National Bank,

www.pvnbank.com,

(308)632-7004

Nevada

Bankwest of Nevada,

(702)248-4200

First National Bank,

(775)289-4441

First Security Bank of Nevada,

(702)952-6000

New Hampshire

Bank of New Hampshire,

www.banknh.com,

(603)624-6600

First Colebrook Bank,

(603)237-5551

New Jersey

Hudson United Bank (formerly Farmers & Merchant Bank NB of Bridget),

www.hudsonunitedbank.com,

(856)451-222

Minotola National Bank,

www.minotola.com,

(856)696-8100

Skylands Community Bank,

(908)850-9010

New Mexico

Valley National Bank, (505)753-2136

Community First Bank (formerly Western Bank),

(505)527-6200

The Citizens Bank of Clovis,

www.citizensbankofclovisnm.com,

(505)769-1911

New York

Wyoming County Bank,

www.wycobank.com,

(716)786-3131

1st National Bank of Scotia,

www.firstcotia.comm,

(518)370-7200

National Bank of Geneva,

www.nbgenea.comm,

(315)789-2300

North Carolina

East Carolina Bank,

(252)925-9461

Four Oaks Bank & Trust Company,

www.fouroaksbank.com,

(919)963-2177

Yadkin Valley Bank & Trust Co.,

(336)526-6301

North Dakota

Kirkwood Bank & Trust Co.,

(701)258-6550

First Western Bank & Trust Co.,

www.fwbt.com,

(701)852-3711

Ohio

Community First Bank & Trust Co.,

www.comfirst.com,

(419)394-3366

First National Bank of Shelby,

(419)342-4010

Sutton State Bank,

www.suttonbank.com,

(419)426-3641

Oklahoma

First Bank & Trust Co.,

www.wagnoer.net/firstbank.htm,

(918)485-2173

First National Bank & Trust Co.,

www.fnada.com,

(580)332-5132

Landmark Bank,

(580)436-1117

Oregon

Security Bank,

www.fbhc.com,

(541)267-5356

Bank of Salem,

(503)585-5290

Pennsylvania

Pioneer American Bank,

www.pioneeramerican.com,

(570)342-8135

First National Bank of Leesport,

www.leesportbank.com,

(610)926-2161

Old Forge Bank,

www.oldforgebankpa.com,

(570)457-8345

Rhode Island

Washington Trust Co.,

www.washtrust.com,

(401)351-6240

Fleet Bank,

www.fleet.com,

(401)278-600

South Carolina

Bank of Travelers Rest,

(864)834-9031

Bank of York,

www.bankofyork.com,

(803)684-2265

Horry County State Bank,

(843)756-6333

South Dakota

Farmers State Bank,

www.farmersstatebanksd.com,

(605)648-3683

Merchants State Bank,

(605)925-4222

Tennessee

First Community Bank of East Tennessee,

(423)272-5800

First State Bank,

(901)475-5000

Volunteer Bank & Trust Co.,

(423)265-5001

Texas

First Bank of Conroe N.A.,

www.fboc.com,

(409)760-1888

First Commercial Bank,

www.1cb.com,

(830)379-8390

Heritage Bank,

www.bankheritage.com,

(972)935-5000

Utah

GE Capital Financial,

www.ge.com,

(801)517-5000

Wright Express Financial Services Corp.,

www.wrightexpress.com,

(801)270-8166

Vermont

Union Bank,

www.unionbankvt.com,

(802)888-6600

Community National Bank,

www.communitybank.com,

(802)334-7915

Virginia

Chesapeake Bank,

www.chesbank.com,

(804)435-1181

F & M Bank--Massanutten,

www.fm-mass.com,

(540)434-6761

Powell Valley National Bank,

www.powellvalleybank.com,

(540)346-1414

Washington

Security State Bank,

www.ssbwa.com,

(360)736-2861

Bank of Whitman,

www.bankofwhitman.com,

(509)397-4629

West Virginia

Traders Bank,

(304)927-3340

Calhoun Banks,

www.calhounbank.com,

(304)354-6116

Wisconsin

F & M Bank Winnebago County,

www.fmbanks.com,

(920)766-1717

F & M Bank Waushara County,

(920)787-3351

Wyoming

First State Bank of Wheatland,

(307)322-5222

First National Bank of Buffalo,

www.fnb-buffalo.com,

(307)684-2555

Other Small Business Friendly Banks

The SBA studied the top multibillion-dollar bank holding companies with domestic assets of more than $10 billion. The SBA ranked these companies in order of their "small-business friendliness."

1. **Wells Fargo & Co.,**

   www.wellsfargo.com

2. **Bank of America Corp.,**

   www.bankofamerica.com

3. **Bank One Corp.,**

   www.bankone.com

4. **U.S. Bancorp,**

   www.usbank.com

5. **Chase Manhattan Corp.,**

   www.chase.com

6. **Colonial BancGroup Inc.,**

   www.colonialbank.com

7. **National City Corp.,**

   www.national-city.com

8. **CitiGroup Inc.,**

   www.citigroup.com

9. **BB & T Corp.,**

   www.bbandt.com

10. **First Union Corp.,**

    www.flrstunion.com

11. **KeyCorp,**

    www.key.com

12. **Regions Financial Corp.,**

    www.regionsbank.com

13. **Suntrust Banks Inc.,**

www.suntrust.com

14. Fleet Financial Group (merged with BankBoston Corp.),

www.fleet.com

15. Union Planters Corp.,

www.unionplanters.com

16. First American Corp. (merged with AmSouth

Bancorporation),

www.fanb.com

17. Firstar Corp.,

www.firstar.com

18. PNC Bank Corp.,

www.pncbank.com

19. Wachovia Corp.,

www.wachovia.com

20. Synovus Financial Corp. ,

www.synovus.com

21. Marshall & Ilsley Corp.,

www.micorp.com

23. Huntington Bancshares Inc.,

www.huntington.com

24. Southtrust Corp.,

www.southtrust.com

25. M & T Bank Corp.,

www.mandtbank.com

26. **LaSalle National Bank,**

www.lasallebanks.com

27. **AmSouth Bancorporation (merged with First American Corp.),**

www.amsouth.com

28. **Compass Bancshares,**

www.compassbank.com

29. **Hibernia Corp.,**

www.hibernia.com

30. **Zions Bancorporation,**

www.zionsbank.com

31. **First Tennessee National Corp.,**

www.ftb.com

32. **Comerica Inc.,**

www.comerica.com

33. **First Security Corp. (merged with Wells Fargo & Co.),**

www.firstsecuritybank.com

34. **HSBC Bank USA,**

www.hsbc.com

35. **Union Bank of California,**

www.uboc.com

36. **Mellon Bank Corp.,**

www.mellon.com

37. **Fifth Third Bancorp,**

www.53.com

38. Commerce Bancshares Inc. ,

www.commercebank.com

39. Summit Bancorp,

www.summitbank.com

40. Allfirst,

www.allfirst.com

41. BankBoston Corp. (merged with Fleet Financial Group),

www.bkb.com

42. Associated Banc.Corp.,

www.associatedbank.com

43. Old Kent Financial Corp.,

www.oldkent.com

44. North Fork Bank (formerly North Fork Bancorporation),

www.northforkbank.com

45. Bank of New York Co. Inc.,

www.bankofny.com

46. Pacific Century Financial,

www.boh.com

47. BancWest Corp,

www.bancwestcorp.com

48. Harris Trust & Savings Bank,

www.harrisbank.com

49. Michigan National Bank,

www.michigannational.com

50. Northern Trust Corp.,

www.ntrs.com

52. TCF Financial Corp.,

www.tcfbank.com

53. State Street Corp.,

www.statestreet.com

54. J.P. Morgan & Co. Inc.,

www.jpmorgan.com

55. Bankers Trust Corp. (acquired by Deutsche Bank),

www.bankerstrust.com

Appendix II

Resources for Women and Minority Owned Non-Medical Home Care Businesses

Government resources

Women:
National Women's Business Council:
http://www.nwbc.gov/

The NWBC advises and counsels the president and Congress on economic issues of importance to women business owners. Look around this site for information on legislation, business research and free publications, such as the "1999 Guide to Contracting with women" (http://www.nwbc.gov/BestPractices.PDF). This 97-page report identifies model programs that have been effective in increasing competitive contracting opportunities for women-owned firms.

Office of Women's Business Ownership:
http://www.sbaonline.sba.gov/womeninbusiness/

This SBA site provides links to venture capital, procurement and lending programs.

SBA's Online Women's Business Center:
http://www.onlinewbc.org/

The SBA has put a lot of effort into this site. Travel to the "Market Mall" to find training and information on a wide variety of marketing, public relations and advertising topics. Visit the "Finance Center" for information on banking, accounting and more. The "Management Institute" aims to help you lead your company into the future, develop good business relationships and sharpen your management skills. "Technology Tower" offers information on computers and the Internet, and "Procurement Place" provides tools to compete and succeed in the federal marketplace.

Minorities:

Equal Employment Opportunity Commission:
http://www.eeoc.gov
The EEOC enforces the federal laws that prohibit employment discrimination on the basis of a person's race, color, religion, sex, national origin, age or disability. The commission's site has a "Quick Start -- Employers" section that offers a basic introduction to employers' rights and responsibilities. Of special interest to small businesses is the "Small Business Information" page, which answers Frequently Asked Questions about small companies' compliance with discrimination laws.

Minority Business Development Agency:
http://www.mbda.gov/
Part of the U.S. Department of Commerce, MBDA offers a wide range of services to minority businesses, including the "Phoenix Database" of minority-owned U.S. companies, which helps match companies with contracts, loans, partnerships and other business opportunities via e-mail. The Online Resources page provides downloadable reports and data on the emerging minority marketplace, while the Virtual Business Centers provide a wealth of information for minority entrepreneurs looking for technical, financial, business and market assistance in areas such as international trade and franchising.

Minority and Enterprise Department:
http://www.sba.gov/med/

Small Disadvantaged Business:

http://www.sba.gov/sdb/index.html

These two SBA sites provide information on the 8(a) Business Development Program and the Small Disadvantaged Business Certification Program. 8(a) offers a wide range of assistance to disadvantaged firms while SDB Certification gives companies an edge when competing for federal contracts.

Office of Government Contracting and Minority Enterprise Development:

http://www.sba.gov/gcmed/index.html

Visitors can learn about various government programs designed to help small, disadvantaged and women-owned businesses obtain government contracts and excel.

Office of Small Business and Minority Affairs:

http://www.dol.gov/dol/osbma/welcome.html

The Department of Labor created the OSBMA to give small, disadvantaged businesses and minority institutions the opportunity to take part in government contracting and grant activities. The office conducts outreach programs and seminars for small minority businesses, and visitors can find publications, a list of administered laws and more on the Web site.

Other resources

Women:

American Business Women's Association:
http://www.abwa.org/

Founded in 1949, the ABWA provides networking, educational and career development opportunities for businesswomen across the country. The site offers advice articles, news about upcoming conferences and classes, information about local ABWA councils, and the "Company Connection," a special networking and support section for business owners.

Columbia College Center for Women Entrepreneurs:
http://www.businessforwomen.org/
Columbia's center offers a wealth of information for the woman entrepreneur, from online discussions and classes, to classified ads for business services and access to business research.

The Forum for Women Entrepreneurs:
http://www.fwe.org/
FWE is an entrepreneurial organization for women building and leading high-growth technology and life sciences companies. Here, women can consult a resources section rich in advice from FWE members. Visitors can read about giving a venture-funding presentation and creating a "killer" business plan, and also scroll through a list of investment counsellors. The site also includes a monthly newsletter and links to local chapters.

National Association of Women Business Owners:
http://www.nawbo.org/
NAWBO describes itself as the only dues-based national organization representing the interests of female entrepreneurs in all types of businesses. The organization currently has more than 75 chapters. Members can take part in online discussion forums, network with other members, access educational opportunities, read articles and take part in NAWBO's electronic lobbying efforts.

National Foundation for Women Business Owners:
http://www.nfwbo.org/
This non-profit research organization studies women business owners and their companies worldwide. Visitors to the site can read key facts about women-owned businesses, browse recent research results and access a list of related links. Check out the "Research" tab for a long list of studies conducted by NFWBO.

National Women Business Owners Corporation:
http://www.nwboc.org/
This national non-profit corporation was established to help women-owned businesses compete for corporate and government contracts. The NWBOC network offers electronic access to detailed information about corporate, federal, state and local government contracting.

Organization of Women in International Trade:

http://www.owit.org

This non-profit organization provides networking and educational opportunities for women involved in international trade. Visitors can search OWIT for job openings, register on the site as a speaker, read the latest international trade news, view a calendar of events and find the nearest chapter.

Springboard: Women's Venture Capital Forum:

http://www.springboard2000.org/

Springboard 2000 is a national initiative designed to expand the investment channels for women entrepreneurs and encourage investments in women-led firms by investors across the nation. Here, you can learn about the Springboard venture forum series, which showcases women entrepreneurs in New England, the Mid-Atlantic and Silicon Valley. You can also read about the latest forum, sign up for future forums, and learn about women-focused venture funds and angel investment groups.

Women's Business Enterprise National Council:

http://www.wbenc.org/

WBENC provides a nationally recognized standard of certification for women-owned business across the country. Here, women can find information on certification as well as news about contracting with companies and government agencies.

Women Incorporated:

http://www.womeninc.com/

Women Incorporated is a non-profit organization designed to improve the business environment for women. This site provides articles from the Women's Biz Journal, an online member directory to facilitate business-to-business sales among woman-owned companies, online discussion forums, and information about becoming certified as a Women's Business Enterprise.

Minorities:

Disabled Businesspersons Association:

http://www.web-link.com/dba/dba.htm

This organization helps disabled entrepreneurs and professionals maximize their potential in the business world.

Inroads:

http://www.inroadsinc.org/

This organization places talented minority youths in businesses, preparing them for corporate and community leadership.

National Black Business Council Inc.:
http://www.nbbc.org/index.html
The NBBC is a non-profit organization that actively supports the
creation and advancement of black-owned businesses. The site
features an overview of the council, a calendar of events and an
online help form for requesting additional information.

National Minority Business Council:
http://www.nmbc.org/
NMBC provides business assistance, educational opportunities,
seminars, purchasing exchanges, mentoring, business listings and
related services to hundreds of businesses across the United
States.

National Minority Supplier Development Council:
http://www.nmsdcus.org
This organization certifies minority-owned businesses and then
matches them with more than 3,500 corporate businesses that
want to purchase goods and services from minority-owned firms.
The site provides its members with a database of more than 15,000
minority businesses, links to the home pages of affiliated regional
councils throughout the United States, information about business
opportunity fairs and more.

www.ingramcontent.com/pod-product-compliance
Lightning Source LLC
Chambersburg PA
CBHW071506140726
47997CB00005B/1876